McSweeney's

THE McSWEENEY'S JOKE BOOK OF BOOK JOKES

Based in San Francisco, McSweeney's publishes books, a monthly magazine called *The Believer*, and two quarterlies—one for short fiction (*McSweeney's*), and one for short films (*Wholphin*). Since 2002, McSweeney's has shared space with 826 Valencia, a nonprofit educational center for Bay Area youth, and has helped support its six sister centers in other cities

www.mcsweeneys.net

ALSO FROM McSWEENEY'S

Mountain Man Dance Moves: The McSweeney's Book of Lists

Created in Darkness by Troubled Americans:
The Best of McSweeney's Humor Category

McSweeney's Enchanted Chamber of Astonishing Stories

McSweeney's Mammoth Treasury of Thrilling Tales

McSweeney's Quarterly Concern

The Believer

Wholphin

The McSweeney's Joke Book
of Book Jokes

THE McSWEENEY'S
JOKE BOOK OF
BOOK JOKES

From the editors of
McSweeney's

VINTAGE BOOKS

A Division of Random House, Inc.

New York

A VINTAGE BOOKS ORIGINAL, APRIL 2008

Library of Congress Cataloging-in-Publication Data:
The McSweeney's joke book of book jokes / from the
editors of McSweeney's. —1st ed.
p. cm.
ISBN 978-0-307-38733-2
1. Books—Humor. 2. Literature—Humor. I. McSweeney's.
PN6231.B62M37 2008
818'.5402080357—dc22
2007042792

www.vintagebooks.com

Printed in the United States of America
10 9 8 7 6 5 4 3 2 1

The McSweeney's Joke Book
of Book Jokes

AN INTRODUCTION TO A BOOK OF BOOKISH HUMOR FROM McSWEENEY'S

by John Hodgman

Greetings, readers of books.

My name is John Hodgman.

It is my great pleasure to introduce you to this book of bookish humor from McSweeney's. It is my great pleasure, and also my compulsion, for as you know, I am in their debt.

It was, after all, in the pages of *McSweeney's*, as well as in the virtual un-pages of mcsweeneys.net, where I finally switched sides, as it were, giving up my gainful employ as a professional literary agent and becoming instead a writer.

And so it was that I first discovered the incredible, untapped commercial potential of the genre that would come to be known as "EXTREMELY BOOKISH, VERGING ON TERMINALLY NERDY, LITERARY HUMOR," which would become something of a hallmark of McSweeney's and which, for me, would become, quite literally, a gold mine.

In the year 2000, after just the first appearance of my occasional advice column "Ask a Former Literary Agent," I was able to buy three houses for no money down, plus a boat with beautiful women on it.

After my second appearance, I had to sell those things because it turns out I did not make any money on my first appearance. But I was mentioned on a blog (though we didn't call them "blogs" back then, but "websites" or "bsites").

Yes, there were ups and downs, but now, THERE ARE ONLY UPS. As you may know, I now have a lucrative book writing career cracking wise about the pathetic fallacy and the thirty-six dramatic situations, and I regularly appear on television making jokes about Harold Bloom.

And as you page through this book, you will find the work of similar pioneers in the bookish nerd-humor field, and you will say to yourself: Hey! I have an English degree and/or an MFA in poetry and know a few good Raymond Carver jokes. How did I miss out on this amazing creative moment and FIRST-CLASS PLATINUM MONEY TROUGH? I wish I could hear from someone who got in on the ground floor and could show me how it is done.

Well guess what? I was there, literally. And I am here to help.

One question I am commonly asked at my many seminars is this: What is the secret of literary parody?

And my answer is always the same: SHUT UP, AND GET OUT.

Can you imagine anything more tiring than a book of droll, pitch-perfect emulations of a particular genre or narrative voice? Just writing that sentence made me tired. AND ANGRY.

(Similarly, there will be many people in your life who will attempt to explain to you the difference between "parody" and "satire," and all of them should be shunned, as they are loathsome people.)

Whatever the intent of such emulation, the result is usually not lasting and usually not funny.

By contrast, the pieces gathered within are not send-ups or emulations. Jared Bloom's fragment of the very authorized biography of Steven Seagal does not rely on your knowledge of the tropes of celebrity biography in order to be funny; it merely requires that you have some familiarity with ass-kicking. Similarly, Tim Carvell's "Unpublished Coda to Harper Lee's *To Kill a Mockingbird*" asks only that you find the image of Atticus Finch killing a monkey funny. AND ALL HUMANS DO.

Rather, these are all original pieces of humorous writing that are joined together merely by their appreciation of the intrinsic and unique hilariousness of books.

The next question I often get in my seminars is this: Are books themselves an arbitrary subject for humor, or is there something intrinsically and uniquely hilarious about books and book culture?

To which I reply: WHAT DID I JUST TELL YOU? WHAT IS WRONG WITH YOU PEOPLE?

We all know that books are funny. First, they are made of paste and cloth, which is funny, as is the fact that people still buy and read them.

Also, books connote a sort of intellectual stuffiness, which is always easy and appealing to make fun of. It's humanizing. Jean-Paul Sartre was a gloomy genius. When you realize he had a walleye and a clubfoot and a hunched back and a wooden thigh, it's consoling and also very funny.

Another example. It is hilarious that Herman Melville wrote *Moby-Dick*. It is hilarious, too, that he was never recognized for his accomplishment in his lifetime . . . that it would one day be considered a classic, earning praise and fortunes that Melville would never enjoy, due to his being dead. It is hilarious that it has a tattooed cannibal in it named "Queequeg" and also a guy with a peg leg, and what's more, its GODDAMNED TITLE IS *MOBY-DICK*. Priceless. I know, as we all do, that *Moby-Dick* is hilarious, and I HAVEN'T EVEN READ IT.

To borrow a term from Yiddish vaudeville, Melville was a "loser." And this speaks, I think, to the true secret of why books and authors are funny: because they are sad.

They are sad as zeppelins are sad: they wish to soar, but they are using a technology that is old, largely forgotten, and highly flammable. It is this ambition to relevance that makes books and zeppelins funnier than blimps, which you will agree are merely pathetic, and, since they do not have rigid siding, mushy.

As I mentioned before, some years ago I worked at a literary agency. Short of prowling the aisles of the Strand, there is nothing to remind you more of the sadness of books than working at a literary agency. The agency had once been a nineteenth-century bank, and piled in its various odd corners and down its long halls were books by our clients, most of them long out of print, each one once a dream that had briefly glimmered and then came to rest and molder here, forgotten. I seem to recall that many of them were collections of semischolarly essays on the subject of *Star Trek*. But that was just chance and the particular taste of this agency.

Regardless of their *Star Trek* content, most books are personal. Most books take time. Most books want to be remembered and to contribute to the culture, a culture that was beginning to care about books less and less. And all of these books were forgotten.

And these were just the published books. You can imagine how many more came to us for consideration that would never be published, often accompanied by a photograph of the author, smiling, hoping, maybe holding a quill or a dog.

Aspiring authors, let me confirm your deepest fears: yes, we made fun of you. We junior members of the agency would put your photos up on a bulletin board and laugh and laugh.

We would take your manuscripts once a week into the vault and burn them there while dancing. We were not just being cruel: it was a ritual, an exorcism. As you can imagine, publishing's lowest ranks are larded with aspiring writers, and we feared your manuscripts and your desperation because we were afraid it would curse us.

And then when the burning was done, we would collapse in a crazed heap and sleep for days. Thinking back, if I were to do it all again, I probably would leave the vault door open a crack. But those were the crazy days, the go-go, set-a-fire-in-an-airtight-vault midnineties. And I was drunk.

Now, it never came to pass that we burned a manuscript of twee bookish humor, because honestly, who would have been crazy enough to write such a thing?

But things began to change. When the Internet began to take hold, suddenly everyone could publish their essays on *Star Trek*, and they would be in print forever.

And then came McSweeney's. And like a simile-as-yet-to-be-determined-connoting-great-and-sudden-speed-and-power, a generation of young writers found a venue that was not controlled by people like me, who had access to big publishers and airtight vaults, a venue that would not bog their creativity down with slow pub dates, editing, and cash payments.

And the result, almost from the beginning, was the kind of work you hold in your hands now: relentlessly smart and inventive, often unbearably funny, and largely preoccupied with the fact that, other than allowing us to make fun of them, our English degrees were pretty useless.

Soon enough I gave up my publishing job and rituals and joined fates with the authors you now find collected within. And this book is testament to a very curious fact, the one thing related to McSweeney's that may be termed actually "ironic": that while books are more and more marginalized and zeppelin-like in our culture (except for books by Rachael Ray and Tim Gunn and Barry Sudoku), the love of writing and stories—including those compact little stories we call "jokes"—and all of that which we might call bookishness—would seem to be more alive than ever, and NOT EVEN I CAN STOP IT.

And we all know what that means: CASH MONEY ON THE TABLE. So read this book, study its lessons, and go out there and make a fortune. IF I COULD DO IT, you can. Now please get away from me.

That is all.

THE RECRUITMENT OF HARRY POTTER

by Craig Borman

RE: Harry Potter campus visit
IMPORTANCE: High

Hey, all,

It's twenty-four hours until the big visit, and I hope by now everyone understands how pivotal this weekend is for us. Harry Potter has some off-pitch issues, but he's the best seeker I've seen in eighty years. Vic Krum says Potter can do things on a broom that he can only dream of, and Krum didn't win MVP at worlds last year because the committee pulled his name out of a hat. And if that's not enough, word from management is that it's all of our asses if he signs with someone else.

The good news is that it sounds like it's between us and Puddlemere, if Potter decides to play at all. We have to do whatever it takes to ensure we have a commitment before he leaves on Sunday. Let me say that again—*whatever it takes.* Do things I don't want to know about if you have to, but let's be sure he signs on the dotted line.

He and the Weasley kid are flying in on Friday. We're going to have to make an offer to both—Richardson, relax, nobody's going to take your job. We'll sit Weasley on the bench or ship him to the minors when the time comes, but we have to get him to commit to have any chance at all with Potter.

Wootton and Owen, Weasley's your responsibility for the weekend. Show him the cheerleaders, the parties . . . hell, apparate him to India and show him the Taj Mahal for all I care, just make sure he thinks we're recruiting him regardless of whether Potter signs or not. If it means hiring some extra "talent" to seal the deal, whip out the credit card and do whatever it takes. But it probably won't be a tough sell. Weasley loves Quidditch and would probably go over to the Dark Lo— to He Who Must Not Be Named for a chance at the pros.

Potter is going to be a lot tougher. Bell says Potter wants to be an Auror, so we should definitely break out the academics among the season-ticket holders. Sell that we're the closest team to the Ministry of Magic, and that we're his best option if he wants to play at all, since he'll be able to manage the classwork and practice. Hey, if he actually can, more power to him.

Tell him we will absolutely pull Snape's season tickets if that's any concern at all. Hell, go ahead and do that anyway. Guy gives me the willies.

Don't worry—by all accounts Quidditch is Potter's main obsession. Well, that and the whole feud thing, but let's not bring that up unless he broaches the subject. (None of us have the Dark Mark, right? If any of you do, be sure to wear your long-sleeve jersey.) You know he'll love the facilities—the broom deal with Nike Magic, the state-of-the-art pitch, the sellout crowds . . .

As for the entertainment . . . I'm at a loss. We know he has commitment issues and isn't looking for anything serious, but that's about it. He dated that Chang girl for a while—the one who's probably going to wind up signing with Cardiff—and Weasley's sister. And Slughorn said there might have been something going on between Potter and some weirdo—her father runs the *Quibbler* or something. Bottom line is, I have no clue what type of girls he'd be interested in. But, for the love of Gryffindor, don't let the entertainment for Potter and Weasley overlap—the last thing we need is Weasley seeing Potter snogging another girl, and both of them getting all bent out of shape.

I'll be in charge of the Potter visit (except for entertainment—I'm looking for volunteers for that gig). We all know the sad story—dead parents, dead godfather, dead headmaster. He's in need of a father figure, and I'm willing to risk it. Yeah, a lot of people close to Potter wind up dead, but it's worth the danger for someone who's guaranteed to catch the snitch every time out. If it gets me a championship ring, I'll take all the Unforgivable Curses with a smile on my face.

Oh, and for the love of Gryffindor, don't let slip that we had Malfoy in last week. Word has it that they don't much like each other, so keep it on the down-low.

Let's do it.

—Coach

SOCIAL SECURITY DENIES GREGOR SAMSA'S DISABILITY CLAIM

by Alex St. Andrews

Important Notice
GREGOR SAMSA Is Not Eligible for SSI
We are writing about GREGOR SAMSA's claim for Supplemental Security Income (SSI) payments. Based on a review of his/her medical condition, he/she does not qualify for SSI payments on this claim. This is because he/she is not disabled or blind under our rules.

The Decision on GREGOR SAMSA's Case
You listed the following impairment(s) on your SSI application:
I AM A GIGANTIC COCKROACH
DEPRESSION
BACK PAIN

You said the above impairment(s) affected you in the following way(s):
I CANNOT STAND OR WALK UPRIGHT OR SPEAK ANY
HUMAN LANGUAGE.

I CANNOT HANDLE OR MANIPULATE OBJECTS WITH MY
MANY LEGS OR ANTENNAE.

WHEN I AM ON MY BACK I HAVE DIFFICULTY RIGHTING
MYSELF.

MY FAMILY HAS IMPRISONED ME IN MY ROOM AND IS
FEEDING ME SCRAPS.

The following report(s) were used to decide this claim:
- You did not show up for your Consultative Exam. We scheduled
an appointment with an examining physician at our expense. You
were asked if you required a taxi or other arranged transportation
to the exam.
- We received no medical records related to your alleged condition(s)
of I AM A GIGANTIC COCKROACH, DEPRESSION,
BACK PAIN.

Doctors and other trained staff looked at this case and made this
decision. They work for the state but used our rules. The following
findings were made:
- You are not engaged in any substantial gainful activity.
- Your impairment causes more than minimal limitations.
- Although your impairment(s) result in some problems for you,
which are more than minimal, they do not equal any of the
impairments listed in Table 2 of Appendix 1 to Subpart P of
Chapter 20, Part 404 of Federal Regulations ("the Listings").
- You are not able to perform your previous employment. You
listed the following job(s) in your work history report:
  TRAVELING SALESMAN
- We have determined that your impairment prevents you from
continuing in your previous employment, because you cannot
handle or finger your sample cases, you cannot speak any human

language, and your customers will be frightened by your monstrous clicking mandibles.

- You are able to perform other work which exists in substantial numbers in the national economy. A vocational expert was consulted, and determined that your Residual Functioning Capacity (RFC) allows you to perform the following jobs:

STAPLING MACHINE OPERATOR
NUCLEAR WASTE MANAGEMENT
ENTERTAINER (foreign cinema, circus)
TAX PREPARER

If You Disagree with the Decision

If you disagree with this decision, you have the right to appeal. We will review your case and consider any new facts you have. You have to ask for an appeal in writing. We will ask you to sign a form SS-561-U2, called "Request for Reconsideration." If you cannot sign your name, you may mark the line with an X, but you must provide two witnesses willing to sign to your identity. If you cannot mark the line with an X, we will provide you with a special identity stamp. If you cannot handle or finger the identity stamp, we will ask you to come into our office and frantically paw at a ream of carbon triplicate paper, but you must provide two witnesses willing to sign to your identity.

If you do call or visit an office, please have this letter with you. It will help us answer your questions. You must have your Social Security card and a current picture ID to enter the building.

Sincerely,

Barnabas Klamm
Regional Commissioner

FROM THE FOUND NOTEBOOKS
OF THE MEMBERS OF
HOMER'S WRITING GROUP

by Sean Carman

Re: "The Odyssey"

II: Another solid story from the group's most prolific member! And we'd barely finished workshopping the *Iliad*! A lot going on here that I like. Nice arc to the story, and I'm heartened you let the plot play a larger role in this one—sustains the dramatic tension, and provides some fascinating twists! Really liked the setting details, e.g., "dawn with her rose-red fingers" and Odysseus's "black-beaked ships." Excellent word economy, as usual.

Overall, good job. My thoughts:

I understand what you are doing with the suitors overstaying their welcome in their pursuit of Odysseus's wife, Penelope—making the reader want Odysseus to make it home so his wife won't marry another, etc. I think you're on the right track, because for this story to work the reader definitely has to want Odysseus to make it home. But is Penelope really going to forsake Odysseus for the offerings of any of these pretenders? The idea seems to undercut her unceasing devotion to him, which you develop quite well. Also, seems a little contrived for the bond between Penelope and battle-hardened Odysseus, direct descendant of Zeus, to be threatened by a rabble of guests overstaying their welcome at a dinner party. With these choices, why wouldn't Penelope simply remain single? Tried to think of a more compelling reason for Odysseus to make it home, but couldn't come up with much...maybe a local conflict threatens Penelope and Odysseus's son, Telemachus, like the battle for Troy but on a smaller scale? (Just make sure you don't mimic the "Trojan horse" incident. As good as that was, it's the kind of thing you can only use once. Bringing it back would seem tired.) Maybe a gang of rogue swineherds kidnaps Penelope and demands Telemachus's sacrifice as ransom? Just some ideas to get you started.

The Cyclops is wonderful! You have such an imagination! A little confused as to why they have to spend so long in the cave, though. Maybe they could feed Cyclops the wine a little earlier, to make him fall asleep sooner? That would quicken Odysseus's escape, cut the scene short, and pick up the pace. Then you could interpose a plot complication on their return to the ship, for a more satisfying denouement.

Having Circe turn Odysseus's men into swine is a great imaginative device. Really sets up a great conflict, esp. given the crew's aching hunger and lack of other food. Still, I wonder if you could do more before Odysseus unmasks Circe's deception? What if, for example, before Odysseus's return one of the crew catches a fleeting glimpse of a fellow warrior in the eyes of one of the swine? That could provide a tender moment, with the crew member unknowingly seeing through Circe's spell, yet one also filled with self-doubt, because the idea of a man transforming into a pig is so naturally ludicrous. See what I mean? Might also raise larger "nature of man" issues not fully explored here, though you're definitely on track.

I love Scylla and Charybdis! Reminded me of all those times there's no easy way out of some difficult situation! Talk about symbolism! And the scene really shows Odysseus's leadership, bravely deciding to sacrifice some of his crew to save the group, etc. Still, why does Scylla snatch up and devour six men, instead of some other number? Yes, you say Scylla has six heads, but you don't explain why the monster has that particular number of heads. Seems like it could easily be four, or ten. Why not twenty? Also, you haven't told us how many men are on the ship. This is a problem throughout, actually—and keeps us from gauging the seriousness of the repeated incidents in which some number of crew meet their doom. With a crew of twelve, the loss of six men would be pretty serious. (How many men does it really take to sail the ship anyway—that's another fact I think the reader needs to know.) But let's say the men on the ship number sixty. Then the loss of six doesn't seem so bad—only 10 percent. See my point? So, if you're going to stick with six heads for Scylla, I think I'd put twenty or so men on the ship at that point. Either way, I think you have to specify, and, anyway, doing so would drive the tension that much deeper.

Oh, also, had no idea what the whole visit to the Kingdom of the Dead was getting at. Interesting, but seems unrelated to the larger story. I'd cut it. Remember—this is a story about one man's attempt to get home. Stay focused on that.

In the final chapters, I like Odysseus's return in the guise of an anonymous vagrant—again, excellent symbolic choice—but the device wears a little thin. Doesn't it seem odd no one suspects anything? It also seems an unnecessarily complicated device for symbolizing the difficulty of becoming reacquainted with a long-lost love. Why not just give us the scene of Odysseus and Penelope reunited? We could see them fumbling with introductions, exchanging embarrassed confessions and revelations, etc. Isn't that the center of the story? Also, I don't buy that Telemachus can't string Odysseus's bow. Let's not forget he's the great-great-grandson of a god. He should be able to string a bow. Maybe he could string it, but not quite as well? Maybe the bow has lost its fabled rigidity, allowing Telemachus to string it for the first time in his life, thereby providing a nice "coming of age" touch? Also, doesn't each suitor's failure even to come close to stringing Odysseus's bow pretty much give away Odysseus's slaughter of them in the end? If you want that to be a surprise, you're going to have to disguise it more cleverly.

On the whole, though, an excellent first draft. Look forward to reading your revisions!

WINNIE-THE-POOH IS MY COWORKER

by John Moe

March 5

Maureen brought the new guy around who's going to be working in our group. After the Jason fiasco, we really could use someone with a little bit of a brain who can keep up on things. This guy's named Winnie and, I don't know, I just have a bad feeling.

March 9

I've been training Winnie for three days now and I'm ready to kill him. I showed him how the spreadsheets are updated on the network, and he just stared at me with this blank expression. I tried to demonstrate the copy machine, but he somehow got his head stuck in one of the slots. I heard his muffled cry of "Oh, bother!" as five of us worked on getting him out. Honestly, is this the best that recruiting could do? Kirk thinks Winnie might be someone's cousin or something. Not a bad explanation, except that we don't have any other yellow bears working here.

March 11

Although he's worthless, everyone loves Winnie. The girls from marketing come by at least a couple of times a day to hang around his cubicle and talk to him. It's not like they respect his work, since he doesn't do any. And I don't think they even respect him. They're just there to be, like, amused. If he were to make a move on one of them, they'd shoot him down so fast. I mean, I don't respect Winnie, either, but at least I keep my distance.

March 15

I gave Winnie this file of research material on Crawford & Horowitz, because I thought he might want to read up on it before the group meeting tomorrow. I'm doing him a favor, right? So I go to get it back from him after lunch and find Winnie sitting on the floor, his hand in a honey jar, and all this paperwork, including the file I need, smeared with thick honey. It's unusable now. I might as well throw it away. Trying not to just go off on the bear, I asked him what the hell happened. He looked all confused and mumbled something about needing "a little postlunch snack." Jesus. Have a freakin' apple, dude.

March 16

Turns out Winnie got honey all over his keyboard as well. So what happens? They bring him a whole new computer. Top-of-the-line machine, too. Here I've been pounding away on this ancient piece of crap for years, and Mr. Honeypot gets a whole new setup. The tech guy who came by said it looked like Winnie had never even turned the old machine on.

March 19

Winnie's friends came by to take him out for lunch today: a little pig, a pissed-off-looking rabbit, an adolescent kangaroo, and a tiger that had to be on coke. Kirk said he saw them at Sbarro eating their slices and looking scared out of their minds. I guess they live way out in the country or something, so I bet the big city blew their minds. Winnie was really happy around them, though. I guess that's good, since he's just been sitting around here moping all the time and staring out the window. He should just leave and spend *all* his time with them.

March 26

Three times this week, Winnie's asked if I want to join him for a picnic or maybe an adventure. No thanks, I tell him very pointedly, I have a lot of work to do. He just sighs and walks off on his own. Silly old bear.

March 30

It's Robin. Walt Robin, the VP of finance. That's how Winnie got the job. Apparently, Winnie has some sort of relationship with Robin's grandson or nephew or something. That's what Kirk told me, and he knows someone in HR. Frankly, I wonder if that's going to be enough to let Winnie stick around. He showed up three hours late today and gave this long story about being chased by bees. Then he brought out another honey pot (his cubicle is covered with empty ones), ate the honey with his hands for a while, and passed out on his desk. I mean, it's so far beyond just not contributing to the workload at this point. It's unhygienic for us, and he's so clearly not healthy. Someone should do something. The little bitch Tami from marketing came by to rub his tummy. Unbelievable.

April 6

Winnie hasn't shown up in three days. I figured he called in sick, but I guess no one's heard anything. He has no phone, so no one's been able to reach him.

April 7

HR asked me to drive out to Winnie's house, since I'm his best friend at the company (sad). I followed the directions and found him in this hollowed-out tree where he apparently lives. He must have offered me honey like twelve times. I have to admit, he looked happier than he ever did at work. I asked if he was planning on coming back to work, but he just said that the office was "quite an adventure" but that he was "glad to be home." He really is a nice guy, but I think it's better for everyone that it's over. He told me to come back and visit sometime and I lied and said I would.

RE: HARDY BOYS
MANUSCRIPT SUBMISSION

by Jay Dyckman

FROM THE DESK OF EUGENE SIMMONS,
EDITOR, SIMON & SCHUSTER
RE: Hardy Boys Manuscript Submission

Dear Sir:

Thank you for your submission of a Hardy Boys mystery. As explained in our submission guidelines, to appeal to today's readers, the Hardy Boys series seeks to bring a contemporary feel to its newest offerings. While we here at Simon & Schuster fully appreciate your efforts to modernize the characters and their adventures, as per our instructions, we have some concerns with your draft.

First and foremost, we are unpersuaded that the subject matter of *The Case of the Secret Meth Lab* is appropriate for our readers. We understand that the manufacturing of narcotics in otherwise bucolic towns has indeed become a problem. That said, we ask you whether Joe Hardy would realistically go undercover and turn into what his brother repeatedly refers to as a "crankhead."

Page 42: While it is important to end each chapter with a cliffhanger, we don't think Frank pacing outside the bathroom door while his girlfriend, Callie, uses a First Response pregnancy test is consistent with the Hardy Boys formula. And he certainly shouldn't be muttering under his breath about doubts that it's even his.

Page 50: Colorful banter between the brothers is, of course, to be expected. Please reconsider, however, whether Joe would tell Frank to "grow a pair." Further, Joe would not dismiss Frank's suggestion to call for help with "Step off, bitch. I know what I'm doing."

Page 57: Lighthearted exchanges with family members have always been a staple of the series. We are having trouble, however, with Aunt Gertrude "tying a few on" and playfully commenting that Frank is "a little light in the loafers." On that note, Frank's adamant attempt to persuade Chet Morton that it is entirely normal for boys to skinny-dip together and his persistent requests for help applying sunblock are probably out of bounds. Question: When did Frank develop a lisp?

Page 60: We encourage including Nancy Drew in the adventure, as it represents great cross-marketing with our other adventure series. We would think it goes without saying, however, that she would not have, nor even contemplate, surgical enhancement. Please delete all references to her "killer rack."

Page 72: While we understand that violence is a necessary part of any adventure series, we think it best that it be downplayed and referred to as delicately as possible. Neither Frank nor Joe has ever "popped a cap" in anyone's posterior and they never will.

Furthermore, we would prefer that Joe's "going medieval" on the villain in this scene explicitly refer to a swift uppercut punch. Period.

Page 80: What's a "k-hole"? Please clarify.

We look forward to receiving your revisions. Please bear in mind that we are well aware of the difficulties of maintaining a proper balance between the series' original concept and the need to reflect current social and cultural norms. That said, your proposal for the next book in the series, *The Mystery of the Hot Girl in the Night-Cam Video*, is likely not headed in the right direction.

Sincerely yours,

Eugene Simmons
Editor

GOOFUS, GALLANT, RASHOMON

by Jim Stallard

Ted, coworker of Gallant:
That freak belonged to the cult of manners. Talk about a true believer. I rode on an airplane with him once, and he wouldn't start eating his meal until everyone was served.

Sheila, Goofus's high-school classmate:
My memory of Goofus is that people saw what they wanted to. I was drawn to him because I sensed he was hurting inside. That's why he put up that wall and was "rude," but who's to say which way is right? It's just a social construct. Is there some cosmic, universal book of manners? I knew they'd find a way to make him pay, though. They always do.

Ronald, middle-school classmate of both:
It was weird; they started at our school at the exact same time. Eighth grade. Everyone thought they were brothers, but it turns out their fathers were just transferred at the same time to the cereal plant in town. Gallant sits down in the front row and starts sucking up to Mr. Anderson, the English teacher. Volunteers for everything, like our literary journal, *Chrysalis*—all that gay stuff.

Shawn, high-school classmate of Goofus:
Goofus—my God, what a bad-boy poseur. I could tell he had picked up his Nietzscheism from a comic book. He would talk about the "Will to Power." But there was also some G. Gordon Liddy mixed in there. He loved doing the candle trick, moving his hand through the flame and pretending he didn't mind the pain. Then I did the same thing with my finger, showing him how full of shit he was.

Natalie, Gallant's high-school friend:
Gallant was one of the few mature guys in our high school. Sensitive. We used to talk about James Taylor during lunch. I thought him the perfect gentleman, and of course my parents loved him. But when someone is polite to the point of having that Moonie quality, it gets to you. Finally it dawned on me that he used that politeness as a way of controlling me. That was what it was all about—he followed the rules because it gave him the advantage.

Alex, high-school teacher of Goofus:
Goofus had a top-notch bullshit detector. Most teenagers think they have one, but his was the real thing, and I'm one of the few teachers who can relate to it. I introduced him to Kerouac, Bukowski, Burroughs. He acted enthusiastic about writing a paper in which they interacted. But it turned out to be seven pages of... well, I was one of the characters in the scene, which was extremely graphic and not what we agreed on.

Paul, Gallant's college acquaintance:
Gallant just didn't get it when it came to relating to people. He would say words the "proper" way that no one normal ever does—you know, "Don't act immatoor." Always the authority. One night I'm walking to dinner with him and another student, a friend from England, and we're ragging on each other—he's calling me "Yank" and I'm calling him "Limey." Gallant breaks in to inform us that "Limey" comes from the British navy, eating limes to avoid scurvy, blah, blah, blah. Gee, thanks, Gallant. Dork.

Brandon, junior-college classmate of Goofus:
Was Goofus a rebel? He sure liked to think so. He cultivated that tousled-hair thing. He wouldn't go out unless he thought the hair was prominent enough. I sat in his living room for forty-five minutes once waiting for him to sculpt it into the perfect unkempt shape. But that roughness was skin deep. I knew he'd be easy pickings in a real fight.

Dan, Gallant's college acquaintance:
Gallant would walk into a party and suck all the air out of the room. He would pretend not to be disapproving but he always made a point of commenting on what you were drinking, or how many you had. "You must really like that kind of beer"—until you edged away.

Darlene, ex-wife of Goofus:
I thought I could change Goofus. Remember, I'm a town girl who's never gone anywhere, and I was looking for some excitement. I had a lot to learn about men. With that electronic ankle bracelet, he couldn't leave the house after dark, so it was always me doing the shopping and running last-minute errands. And through all that he was always talking about how oppressed he was. Try raising three kids when your husband won't get off his ass.

Steve, Gallant's college acquaintance:
Gallant's attempts to seem cool were just painful. One time after making some incredibly lame joke he said, "I'm just breaking your balls," and the rest of us almost died laughing.

Shane, Goofus's army buddy:
Goofus loved Jack Daniel's. And Yukon Jack. He always wanted to do snakebites even though I don't think he liked them—just the name. He would do two and then switch to something else.

Brad, Gallant's coworker:
Gallant was the total company man. There's not a buzzword he didn't use to death. We're at a strategy meeting one day and he actually says, "If you *fail* to *plan* you *plan* to *fail*." I had to avoid making eye contact with Tony, another coworker, because I knew we would both lose it and get in trouble.

Reverend John Swafford, Gallant's minister:
Gallant was a wonderful addition to our church. He always showed tremendous concern for the members, making inquiries and then letting me know which ones seemed to be having personal problems. If he had just had a little more concern for himself, things would not have turned out the way they did.

Harold, charity-event organizer:
What happened was a disgrace. I put together nice events with the right kinds of people attending. I don't need this kind of publicity.

David, Gallant's coworker:
I don't really understand what pushed Gallant over the edge. Serving from the right rather than the left—who even pays attention to that

stuff? Especially at a fund-raiser. I think Gallant must have been on something. There's a side of him nobody knows. It's weird how everything came full circle, though. It was fate Goofus got assigned to serve that table.

Dean, fellow waiter with Goofus:
Goofus told me in the kitchen he had a bad feeling about that night. It was weird because he's not usually superstitious. I was still in there putting garnishes on the plates when I heard the altercation—I just thought someone was getting chewed out for dropping a tray.

David, deputy mayor:
I'm at the next table. Everything is normal. The waiters are bringing the entrees out and whisking the salads away. Suddenly, this nice-looking man at their table explodes in rage. He screams out, "Right is wrong!" several times at this poor server who's looking at him in shock. Before anyone can move he puts one hand on top of the server's head, the other on his jaw, and just snaps his neck, Delta Force–style. Then he sits back down and puts his napkin in his lap.

Evan, Gallant's coworker:
I was sitting across from Gallant. Goofus was baiting him—he was looking right at me with this smirk on his face while he set the plate down. Well, he got a reaction all right. I hope Goofus is happy wherever he is—where exactly do scum go when they die?

George, Gallant's coworker:
Wow—a life sentence. Normally, I'd say Gallant wouldn't last a week on the inside. But I definitely can imagine him being very helpful to some inmate, if you get me.

Harold, cemetery custodian:

Goofus's tombstone is not marked well and is hard to find, but the teenage kids have started making pilgrimages to it. They go there and get drunk and weepy. I find their beer cans and wine bottles along with flowers and notes saying stuff like "You spoke the truth and they killed you for it." I'm thinking: You want to make him out to be your hero, go crazy, I don't care. Just don't leave your crap all over the ground for me to clean up. Didn't anybody ever teach these kids manners?

PERHAPS I SHOULD STOP NAMING THE PROTAGONISTS IN MY SEMI-AUTOBIOGRAPHICAL FICTION AFTER MYSELF

by Teddy Wayne

The Prince of Wall Street

It was simple, yet deviously efficient . . . all he needed to do was route the slush fund to his Cayman Islands account, let it sit there for sixty business days, then reroute it back to his mainland account with Citibank—and no one would be the wiser, least of all the IRS. He reclined in his Aeron chair overlooking the financial district with the satisfaction that comes from duping the U.S. government and knowing your name is Teddy Wayne and your Social Security number is 635-00-4923.

Adulterous Bodies

Was he really unrolling his coworker Melissa's stockings in the supply room during the office Christmas party while his girlfriend of six months, Valerie, mingled just outside? Valerie was vindictive and violent, a hot-tempered Mediterranean vixen; if she ever found out, she would surely take advantage of his severe allergy to peanuts and slip a fatal amount into his food. "But she doesn't know about the peanuts—yet," he thought to himself with relief. "You're safe for now, Teddy Wayne."

A Perfect Murder

He had disposed of all the evidence and cemented his alibis; there was no possible way he could be caught. "Well, Glen Markson," he said to the night wind as he dumped the cold body in the East River near Fortieth Street at 1 a.m. on the night of June 12, "consider yourself the victim of a perfect murder, by none other than Teddy Wayne of 553 East Thirty-seventh Street, Apt. 8F."

Invisible Viruses

He had every sexually transmitted disease known to man that was not immediately apparent to onlookers: gonorrhea, syphilis, HPV, you name it, plus several that had not yet been classified by the CDC. And he was about to hit the Manhattan singles bars full steam, ready with a smile and his standard pickup line: "What's your name? Mine is Teddy Wayne."

Teddy Wayne: Terrorist Mastermind

Here are three things I want to do: assassinate the president; detonate a bomb aboard a 747; and shout "Fire!" in a crowded theater. After everybody flees a Wednesday matinee of *Mamma Mia!* I will cackle and exclaim, "You were all fooled by terrorist mastermind Teddy Wayne." Then I really will set the theater on fire, because musicals are stupid. The first two things will be harder to pull off, though, especially since the no-fly list now includes "Teddy Wayne."

Guantánamo Nights

Fuck.

FOLLOWING MY CREATIVE-WRITING TEACHER'S ADVICE TO WRITE "LIKE MY PARENTS ARE DEAD"

by Ellie Kemper

from "Autumn Days Are Fleeting"
There was a slight nip in the air, and I pulled my anorak closer. The leaves were beginning to turn. Orange, brown, bright yellow. Autumn, I thought. I inhaled deeply, imagining the crisp air filling my lungs. Oh, God. I miss Mom. Why did you take her from me, God? Why did she have to die? She is gone.

from "Seven Days, Five of Them Working"
I agreed with Cynthia. I did. Four hours would never be enough time to prepare the presentation. There was too much data. There were too many bar graphs. It wasn't our fault. We were told the meeting would be on Thursday; it got bumped back to Wednesday. Oh, God. Wednesday. My dad's favorite day. What was it that he used to call it again? Oh, yeah: Hump Day. I miss Dad so much.

from "Reflections on a Lake"

"You guys go ahead," I told Timothy. "I'll wait for you at the dock." Timothy nodded. Really, what was the point of my going out on the sailboat, feeling like this? I would bring down the entire party. After all, that's how both of my parents died. On a sailboat. Lakes aren't always as placid as you might think. Lakes kill. A lake killed my parents. Five months ago today. That's when they died. That's why they're gone.

from "Comas and Shit"

Sometimes I wonder if my mother is ever coming out of this coma. This is horrible, just sitting here and watching her. This chair is so uncomfortable. It's like she isn't even here. It's like she isn't even alive. It's as though she were just—what's that sound? What does that sound mean? Nurse. Nurse! I think we've lost her. I think we just lost my mom to death.

from "On Death"

Death is inevitable, and everywhere. It will happen to all of us. Just like how it already happened to my parents. I would like to write about something else, but it is nearly impossible. Death fills my every thought. It's not fun to go on living when both of your parents are dead. Especially when you got along really well with both of them, like I did. Sure, we had our tiffs here and there, but, on the whole, we were really polite to one another. How can I write about something as inconsequential as winter snow when I have no parents? It is horrible to live with parents who are dead.

from "Wedding Day"

"He's not here," I told the priest. "My father is not here to give me away." The priest gave me a dirty look. I could feel my face redden with ire. "He's not here," I growled, "because he's dead."

from "Telling Children About Grandparents"

"You don't have any," I told Allison for the fourth time that day. "You don't have any grandparents. Your father died before ever introducing me to his parents, and both of my parents are dead. You don't have a grandparent in the world. Because they are either dead or unknown. In my case, they are dead." Allison began to cry, for the fourth time that day.

from "Me"

It was back to that nagging question: What exactly am I? A mess of bone and flesh. A clump of nails and hair. I am all of those things. But isn't there something more? Hidden in this cage of ribs, deep within these layers of tissue, lurking in these strands of sinew, isn't there a soul? I would like to think so. Otherwise, my parents are just straight-up dead. Deep in the ground, down in the dirt, just...dead. Dead as doornails. Oh, sweet Lord. Please let there be a soul. Please, God. Please don't let my parents just be dead.

THIRTEEN WRITING PROMPTS

by Dan Wiencek

1.

Write a scene showing a man and a woman arguing over the man's friendship with a former girlfriend. Do not mention the girlfriend, the man, the woman, or the argument.

2.

Write a short scene set at a lake, with trees and shit. Throw some birds in there, too.

3.

Choose your favorite historical figure and imagine if he/she had been led to greatness by the promptings of an invisible imp living behind his or her right ear. Write a story from the point of view of this creature. Where did it come from? What are its goals? Use research to make your story as accurate as possible.

4.

Write a story that ends with the following sentence: Debra brushed the sand from her blouse, took a last, wistful look at the now putrefying horse, and stepped into the hot-air balloon.

5.

A wasp called the tarantula hawk reproduces by paralyzing tarantulas and laying its eggs into their bodies. When the larvae hatch, they devour the still-living spider from the inside out. Isn't that fucked up? Write a short story about how fucked up that is.

6.

Imagine if your favorite character from nineteenth-century fiction had been born without thumbs. Then write a short story about them winning the lottery.

7.

Write a story that begins with a man throwing handfuls of $100 bills from a speeding car, and ends with a young girl urinating into a tin bucket.

8.

A husband and wife are meeting in a restaurant to finalize the terms of their impending divorce. Write the scene from the point of view of a busboy snorting cocaine in the restroom.

9.

Think of the most important secret your best friend has ever entrusted you with. Write a story in which you reveal it to everyone. Write it again from the point of view of your friend. Does she want to kill you? How does she imagine doing it? Would she use a gun, or something crueler and more savage, like a baseball bat with nails in it?

10.

Popular music is often a good source of writing inspiration. Rewrite Bob Dylan's "Visions of Johanna" as a play.

11.

Write a short scene in which one character reduces another to uncontrollable sobs without touching him or speaking.

12.

Your main character finds a box of scorched human hair. Whose is it? How did it get there?

13.

A man has a terrifying dream in which he is being sawed in half. He wakes to find himself in the Indian Ocean, naked and clinging to a door; a hotel key card is clenched in his teeth. Write what happens next.

DATELINE: TO CATCH A PREDATOR: HUMBERT HUMBERT

by Jeff Barnosky

CHRIS HANSEN (V.O.)

Our hidden cameras catch our predator as he pulls up in his vintage convertible. Tall, European, and movie-star handsome, this man engaged in a disgusting and vulgar—yet beautifully written and erudite— online conversation with our decoy. After walking with an elegant gait to the front door of our *To Catch a Predator* house, he sticks his head in the door.

HUMBERT HUMBERT

Lo? Lo. Lee. Ta. Light of my life, fire of my loins?

CHRIS HANSEN (V.O.)

The underage girl, who is actually a decoy, calls out to the predator so he will feel secure enough to enter. They have spoken on the phone and chatted on the Internet, where he insisted that she call him Dad.

DECOY

Hey, Dad. What's up? Did you bring condoms?

HUMBERT HUMBERT

Of course, my petulant paramour. I also brought the 45s. What kind of name is Chubby Checker? Is he corpulent?

DECOY

Dunno! I have to change my socks. Why don't you make yourself comfortable?

HUMBERT HUMBERT

The vacuum of my soul awaits your every touch; I am a pulse of pure yearning.

DECOY

Silly! Make yourself comfortable.

CHRIS HANSEN (V.O.)

Our Internet prose artist settles in at our *To Catch a Predator* counter and undoes his tie, making himself comfortable. He takes a cookie from our carefully placed tray. This is when I step in.

CHRIS HANSEN

Enjoying that?

HUMBERT HUMBERT

Quilty?

CHRIS HANSEN

No, Chris Hansen. Would you like to tell me what you're doing here?

HUMBERT HUMBERT

I will try to convey in pitiful blank verse what I want to declaim in sonnets and sestinas. I am permanently festooned by nymphet love.

CHRIS HANSEN

So you're here to have sex with a thirteen-year-old girl?

HUMBERT HUMBERT

I have no illusions. My judges will regard this all as a piece of mummery on the part of a madman with gross liking for the fruit *vert*.

CHRIS HANSEN

Let me ask you this. Did you know that you were asking, on the Internet, a thirteen-year-old girl to "let the beastly and beautiful merge"?

HUMBERT HUMBERT

Do you mean sex play?

CHRIS HANSEN

Did you bring beer?

HUMBERT HUMBERT

Yes.

CHRIS HANSEN

Anything else?

HUMBERT HUMBERT

Transistor radio, poodle skirt, Hula Hoop, Pez, saddle shoes, 45-rpm records, a diaphragm...

CHRIS HANSEN

Is there any reason for you to behave as you do? To be so depraved?

HUMBERT HUMBERT

Picnic, lightning. Also, heart disease.

CHRIS HANSEN (*V.O.*)

At this point, our *To Catch a Predator* cameras come into the room, but Humbert Humbert does not attempt to leave.

HUMBERT HUMBERT

Quilty? Do you recall a little girl called Dolores Haze? Dolly Haze?

CHRIS HANSEN

You're free to go.

HUMBERT HUMBERT

She was my child, Quilty!

CHRIS HANSEN

The person you were speaking to online, DZZLEHZZLE, was actually a thirty-five-year-old man named Stanley.

HUMBERT HUMBERT

Lolita. Lolita. Lolita. Lolita. Lolita. The spoonerette spoke in half-yawns and splutters of mirth.

CHRIS HANSEN

Another decoy. That's our *Perverted Justice* decoy, Joan. She's twenty-six.

HUMBERT HUMBERT

Quilty, I want you to concentrate. You are going to die in a moment. Concentrate. Try to understand what is happening to you.

CHRIS HANSEN (*V.O.*)

His threats were empty. Humbert Humbert simply ran out the door and into the waiting arms of the Fort Worth Police Department. He was arrested on charges of child solicitation, possession of an unregistered handgun, and unfettered lust.

I AM MICHIKO KAKUTANI

by Colin McEnroe

What started as a basically innocent college prank has gotten seriously out of hand, and, at the urging of the small group of people who know the truth, I have decided to come forward and admit it.

I am Michiko Kakutani.

Many people will have a hard time accepting the idea that a basically undistinguished middle-aged white man living in Hartford, Connecticut, is actually the brilliant, acerbic, reclusive, rarely photographed lynxlike *New York Times* book critic and Pulitzer winner.

But I am.

The recent disclosure that Riley Weston changed her name and adjusted her age from thirty-two to nineteen in order to continue writing and acting in network television persuaded me that America is ready to hear my story.

Also, I'm tired of being the skunk at the American literary garden party. Do you know what it took out of me to grab a whip and a chair, to go into a steel cage, and get this whole Toni Morrison tiger under control?

It's not as if I've been able to call in to my regular job at the insurance company and say, "Look, I've been up all night poking holes in the windy, specious, New Age utopian blather of some author you probably never heard of in my capacity as Michiko Kakutani. I'm going to be in a little late."

The whole thing started at Yale in the winter of 1972 when my roommates and I made up the name as an all-purpose coinage.

We'd answer the phone "Kevin? No, he's not here. This is his roommate Michiko Kakutani."

We'd use it as a catchall for any nameless broken part of our stereo: "Aha! The problem's with the michiko kakutani."

We'd use it, I'm embarrassed to say, as a metaphor for onanism.

"What'd you do last night?"

"Had a big date with Michiko Kakutani."

In my junior year, my friend Scott had a job in the registrar's office, so we enrolled Michiko Kakutani in a bunch of classes. I got her through Constitutional Law. Steve took African Art for her. Fred got her an A in Biology.

We also got her into a seminar on Marxist Themes in the Work of the Lake Poets, because it seemed like something she'd like, but then nobody could stand the thought of going, so she took an incomplete.

But Michiko Kakutani was always fundamentally my baby. I thought her up. I gave her life.

One night Fred asked me if I was coming out with him and Peter for late-night hot tuna grinders.

"I'd like to, but Michiko Kakutani has had a long day. She wants to turn in."

There was a long pause.

"Colin," Fred began gingerly, "there is no Michiko Kakutani."

I blew up.

"There is! She's got more guts and brains than all of you jerks put together. And one of these days, she's going to expose American culture for the simpering, self-referential, pretentious fraud that it is!"

After that, my friends started giving me a little more space.

The next semester, Michiko Kakutani's folklore professor abruptly announced the final exams would be oral.

I didn't have to think about what I was going to do. I bought a wig, a pretty silk blouse, and lots of makeup. I was thin already, but I dieted down and wore a girdle. I caused a lot of trouble when I characterized Zora Neale Hurston's work as "an overrated hodgepodge exalted by three generations of self-hating, guilt-ridden white men," but I got an A.

After that, I was Michiko Kakutani whenever I needed to be.

I can hear the reader saying, "Oh Jesus, here comes some kind of weird bend-over 'M. Butterfly' scene."

The reader is wrong. Readers, I have noted, are frequently wrong.

I did not begin leading a secret personal life as Michiko Kakutani, nor did I find it more and more difficult to do the writing required for Michiko Kakutani's life without dressing up as her.

One thing I'm kind of proud of, in fact, is how professionally I handled the Michiko Kakutani side of my life. Once I grasped the fact that she was a serious intellectual force urging the reinstitution of craft and the repudiation of sterile, nihilistic culture, I rid myself of lark and caprice and went at it straight ahead.

I have not dressed up as her more than fifty times in my life, and, to be brutally frank, one reason I've come forward now is that I'm forty-four, and my body is thickening, my metabolism slowing, and getting ready to be Michiko Kakutani now requires three weeks of obsessive exercise, diuretics, and amphetamines.

The last time I did it, for a function at the New York Public Library, I arrived in a state of speed-fueled psychosis, which caused me to wait until Dale Peck was walking down a shadowy corridor and coldcock him. Just turned his fucking lights out.

Looking back, I'm sorry I did that.

But, well, it was Dale Peck. Can I be blamed?

There were mornings when I lay exhausted in my bed, and Alice Shaughnessy, the Sligo-bred housekeeper I inexplicably have, would tiptoe in with coddled eggs and toast points.

"Sure and you've been at it again, sir," she'd gasp. "Herself came out again last night?"

"She reviewed Norman Mailer's silly, self-important, inadvertently comical Jesus novel," I'd groan. "Somebody had to knock that fat bastard down, Alice. Michiko Kakutani was the only one with the spine for the job."

"Sir, it's not my place to say," Alice would falter, "but I worry, sir. I fear you're consorting with dark forces beyond your control, sir."

"Alice, it's a zacked-out, feel-good literary culture of mutually masturbatory blurb writers. Nobody wants to be the turd in the punch bowl. Only Michiko tells the tough truth."

Do I feel bad about the deception? Not really. There's more of this stuff going on than you might suspect. When I interviewed Gore Vidal, he kept peering strangely and fidgeting unhappily, and I began to think he saw through my disguise.

I found out later Gore Vidal regularly sends a body double to interviews. The guy was actually nervous that I might see through his disguise.

I also met, through one of the places that sells me supplies, a woman who did three weeks as Robert James Waller. That one, I hear, is a deal where they rotate new people through at intervals, like Menudo.

Believe me, I know what comes next. Every puny author who ever got his ass kicked by yours truly scuttles out of the woodwork and demands to know how I can make writing with conviction the litmus test when I *was a fake.*

If they were better writers, they would know I was never a fake. That's like saying Batman was a fake (within the reality of the comic, I mean). I mean, is Bruce Wayne more real than Batman?

Somebody else will have to decide. I have a ton of lawn work to do, and I want to get it done before the news breaks, because my neighbor Charlie is the kind of guy who will spend the whole day yelling, "Don't worry, Michi! My wife, Claire, is actually James Wolcott."

The main thing to remember is this: you won't have Michiko Kakutani to kick you around anymore. I'm shutting her down, like Hal in *2001*. Actually, I'd like to write a bunch of reviews pointing out that most human characters in current American fiction are not as fully drawn, as warm-blooded, as humanity laden as Hal. I want to, but you know what would happen? People would say, "There goes Michi again."

But it doesn't seem to matter what I say, and that's why I'm quitting. That and the fact that Dirk Bikkembergs no longer has the brushed-on liquid eyeliner I liked. It was very notice-me.

THE DICK AND JANE READER FOR ADVANCED STUDENTS

by Matthew Kennedy

Dick and Jane went on a picnic. They spread the picnic blanket under a tree. Spot chased butterflies.

Dick thought Jane was pretty. Jane thought Dick was handsome.

Because Jane was polite, she poured lemonade for Dick first.

Dick unpacked a stew with fish in it. It was a dish from his native land. Dick's real name was Roberto. He was from a country called Peru.

Jane asked, "What is that funny smell?" Then she remembered her manners and put on a happy face.

Dick paid attention to Jane. He saw the frown before she remembered to smile.

"It is important to try new things," Dick said. "It is not nice to make fun."

Jane wished she had a boyfriend who grew up in America. Her last boyfriend had seen every episode of *The Brady Bunch*. He also liked to sing the theme song to *The Jeffersons*.

Dick said, "I think you will like it." He held a spoon up to Jane's mouth and raised his eyebrows. He knew she liked it when he acted sexy.

Jane wished Dick would stop the Latin-lover act. A little of that went a long way, especially now that the sex was routine.

Spot ran across the picnic blanket. "Spot, go to sleepy," Dick said. "Go to sleepy." Spot did not want to take a nap. He wanted to see if Jane's poor self-image ruined another date.

Jane wished Dick did not have an accent. After living in Los Angeles for five years, she was a racist.

Dick put the spoon down. He thought, *Jane is being closed minded. That is too bad, because trying new things can make you smarter.*

Jane thought, *Dick is not a very good boyfriend. My friend Mary said he is only a C+, and it is important to get As and Bs in school and in life. However, my high school reunion is next month. If I show up with Mary, the lesbian rumors will start again. I wish boys did not make fun of girls who played sports.*

Dick said, "A penny for your thoughts, Jane."

Jane thought, *Next time I will suggest a movie, so we do not have to talk as much.* However, she did not say it out loud. That would have been very rude.

Jane said, "My mother said if you cannot say anything nice, do not say anything at all."

Dick thought, *Now I know why she did not have a boyfriend for two years.* He did not say it out loud because he knew Jane took kickboxing classes at Crunch.

Jane saw an angry look on Dick's face. She knew she had to cheer him up if she wanted him to attend her high school reunion.

Jane asked, "Would you like a blow job?"

"That would be very nice," Dick said. He remembered why he went out with Jane.

As Dick and Jane lay down in the back of Dick's sport utility vehicle, Spot ate the spicy stew. He wanted to help. Spot knew Jane was a racist who saw the stew as a symbol of Dick's ethnicity. He also knew it added to her deep-seated feelings of shame.

Jane breathed through her nose and thought, *There must be an easier way to keep a man.*

Roberto thought, *Jane got the hint about a more gentle technique. Maybe I will invite her to my company party after all.*

Later, Spot went number two a lot. He wished he had not eaten the stew. Sometimes Jane forgot her chores. That meant Spot did not go for a walk every day.

Spot thought, *I know I should not be a scorekeeper, but Jane makes me mad. Next time I will let her fall into a shame spiral like usual.*

Except for Jane and Spot, everyone had a very good time at the picnic.

KLINGON FAIRY TALES

by Mike Richardson-Bryan

"Goldilocks Dies with Honor at the Hands of the Three Bears"

"Snow White and the Six Dwarves She Killed with Her Bare Hands and the Seventh Dwarf She Let Get Away as a Warning to Others"

"There Was an Old Woman Who Lived in a Shoe with a Big Spike on It"

"The Three Little Pigs Build an Improvised Explosive Device and Deal with That Damned Wolf Once and for All"

"Jack and the Giant Settle Their Differences with Flaming Knives"

"Old Mother Hubbard, Lacking the Means to Support Herself with Honor, Sets Her Disruptor on Self-Destruct and Waits for the Inevitable"

"Mary Had a Little Lamb. It Was Delicious"

"Little Red Riding Hood Strays into the Neutral Zone and Is Never Heard from Again, Although There Are Rumors... Awful, Awful Rumors"

"Hansel and Gretel Offend Vlad the Impaler"

"The Hare Foolishly Lowers His Guard and Is Devastated by the Tortoise, Whose Prowess in Battle Attracts Many Desirable Mates"

THE HISTORY OF THE BELOVED CHILDREN'S BOOK SERIES THE BERENSTAIN BEARS

by Doogie Horner

In Yellowstone Park in 1962, a young child left unattended and smothered in honey was eaten by a grizzly bear.

This child was Bobby Berenstain, three-year-old son of Stan and Jan Berenstain. The tragedy prompted the husband-and-wife team to write their first Berenstain Bears book, a pamphlet entitled *Why All Bears Should Be Slaughtered*. The pamphlet was based on a spoken-word rant of Jan Berenstain's, unofficially called "Untitled: Oh God! AAAAAHHH!" which she delivered spontaneously on finding the bear finishing up the last of its yummy, chubby little honey-coated-kid snack. Adorned with police photos, the pamphlet was a moderate success among park rangers and prompted a follow-up book, entitled *A Bear Ate My Baby*.

A string of books followed, flowing from Jan's manically scribbling pen: *I Told You to Stay in the Car*; *Give Me My Baby Back, Mr. Grizzly*; and *I'm Going to Eat Your Cubs and See How You Like It*. These early books are notable for being written in all caps, without periods.

As anger gave way to crushing despair, subsequent books slowly eased from vitriolic streams of gibberish to tender reflections on life. Since their only child was gone, and since Jan was unable to make love because she was now pretty much dead inside, they fashioned a fictitious family for themselves in their books, and (get this) made that family all *bears*! They even had them living in a place called Bear City! Can you believe that? Talk about crazy!

At first glance, these choices may seem odd, but there are numerous historical precedents. Early civilizations often worshipped the predators that hunted them, in an effort to appease them. The Native Americans respected the bear and sought to become bears themselves through religious ceremonies.

Jan and Stan had been humbled by the Great Bear, and sought to become one with it. In their home, they took to walking around nude on all fours, and Jan stopped shaving her legs. They were eventually shot by the Park Service when they began trying to eat other people's babies.

After the deaths of Jan and Stan, the intellectual property and name of the Berenstain Bears were sold to Dr. Seuss, who sold them to Dalton Trumbo, who wrote the remainder of the series under the pseudonym "Dan and Jan Berenstain" (putting the man's name first— typical), sometimes collaborating with Mario Puzo, most notably on *The Berenstain Bears Get the Gimmies*.

A LOST SCENE INVOLVING LOUIS, A TURKEY CHARACTER CUT DURING THE FINAL EDIT OF *CHARLOTTE'S WEB*

by Ann Asher

"I see where you're going with the 'Some Pig' thing, but don't you think it's so vague that it's not even worth writing?" Louis squawked. "I mean, 'Some Pig'—sure, and there's *some* geese, and *some* rats—it just doesn't convey any real sentiment, does it? What reason would it give me, as a pig farmer, to spare Wilbur? Might as well write 'I Give Up' and be done with it."

Louis pecked the ground once or twice thoughtfully, then scratched at the loose dirt of the barnyard with his scaly feet. No one needed a pedicure more than he. "Listen," Louis continued, "if you really want to save Wilbur, maybe you should think about being a little more aggressive. Send a shiver up their spines, so to speak. I'm thinking of a good, old-fashioned 'Watch Your Back' in the web, or maybe just 'Die' if that's too much for you to manage. Though Mr. Zuckerman might take that the wrong way, think you're encouraging killing the pig. Or—hey!—what about just a picture of the farmer with his head cut off? That would be sure to keep everyone away from the pigpen."

"I'm not much of an artist," said Charlotte.

The turkey coughed a little. "Yes, well. You're not much of a writer, either, but that hasn't stopped you yet, has it?" The other animals stared at Louis with wide, disbelieving eyes, but Charlotte only sighed.

"This has to be done by morning," she reminded him.

"Yes, I know. Precious little time, you're only one small spider." He rolled his eyes. "I'm so helpless!" he mocked while flailing his wings. "With that attitude, you'll never get anything done. Look, I already have a better idea. Why not take some of these dead bugs you're done with and dangle them from nooses made of your web? That's threatening."

"My web is rather sheer. I don't think the nooses would show."

Louis took a step back and eyed the web as if studying a painting. "Hm. In that case, why not throw the bugs at the humans as they pass by? Or some of this manure." He started kicking at whatever piles of manure he could find. The other animals dodged the feces and ran.

"And how will that save Wilbur?" a fleeing lamb asked.

Louis said, "Huh?"

"Thank you for your help, Louis. I'll take it from here," Charlotte said, and began her work, just as the sun started to set. The next morning, all the animals gathered around Charlotte's glorious web, which was sparkling with dew. The words "Eat Turkey" glistened in the morning light.

"What's that say?" Louis asked.

"'Some Pig,'" said Charlotte.

THE FIVE MOST DANGEROUS CHILDREN'S BOOKS EVER WRITTEN, ACCORDING TO SEAN HANNITY

by Brian Danilo

1. *Clifford the Big Red Dog,* by Norman Bridwell

According to a reliable source,* Norman Bridwell, a close personal friend of Karl Marx and adviser to Pol Pot, was a card-carrying member of the American Communist Party. The metaphor is obvious: a big *red* canine teaches children the importance of sharing and working together. (While cleverly ignoring the consequences of such un-American behavior.)

Stories include "Clifford Goes to School" and "Clifford Goes to Work, Where He Organizes a Workers' Revolution." Noticeably absent from the collection of short stories are those resulting from the success of the red menace's machinations, such as "Clifford Institutes a Five-Year Plan" or "Clifford Murders Political Dissidents."

*Former senator Joseph McCarthy

2. *A Christmas Carol*, by Charles Dickens

Charles Dickens, in frequent correspondence with both Michael Moore and Ivan the Terrible, wrote this book with the sole purpose of undermining the capitalist spirit of Christmas. Dickens portrays the patriotic and enterprising Ebenezer Scrooge as a wicked man in need of reform. He further advances the liberal agenda by advocating free health care for Tiny Tim and suggesting that poverty is the result of something other than laziness and stupidity.

Not only does Dickens ignore the Christian element of Christmas, he also glorifies such pagan practices as communicating with the dead and looking into the future. Also, it is highly probable that, while writing *A Christmas Carol*, Charles Dickens planned and executed the assassination of Abraham Lincoln.

3. *Goodnight Moon*, by Margaret Wise Brown

Though the writing is vapid and immature, the book manages to challenge both traditional gender roles and the sanctity of heterosexual marriage. Additionally, lines like "Goodnight cow jumping over the moon" make it clear that Brown, business partner of Susan B. Anthony and confidante of Saddam Hussein, does not support our troops.

It should also be noted that Brown, a known feminist, has a history of subversive behavior. Before her death, Rosa Parks admitted that part of the reason she sat at the front of the bus was that "Margaret was egging me on."

4. *A Wrinkle in Time*, by Madeleine L'Engle

In between orchestrating the French Revolution with Robespierre and bad-mouthing President Bush with the Dixie Chicks, French author Madeleine L'Engle wrote *A Wrinkle in Time*, which centers on a fatherless and troublesome thirteen-year-old girl, Meg Murry. Obviously, L'Engle is implying that single mothers need welfare to properly raise their children.

Meg's mother, a beautiful scientist, represents one of the approximately twenty-four billion welfare recipients in America, who purposely have as many illegitimate children as possible, so they can sit at home collecting welfare and watching *Oprah*, eating chocolate bars and being pregnant.

L'Engle also invaded Poland in 1939.

5. *The Adventures of Huckleberry Finn*, by Mark Twain

A limousine liberal if there ever was one, Huck Finn flouts society's laws and refuses to return stolen property because, after finding a robber's large stash of gold in a cave, he no longer identifies with hardworking middle-class Americans who need their slaves to get by.

Mark Twain, godfather of Joseph Stalin and best man at the wedding of Pontius Pilate, suggests that sometimes it is morally correct to *break the law*. Okay, Mr. Twain. So after we don't return runaway slaves, what's next? Strike for eight-hour workdays and a minimum wage? Burn draft cards?

It should also be noted that Twain, who invented cancer and hates puppies, is not even using his real name. Samuel Clemens, wherever you're hiding, if you have any integrity, you will appear on my show and defend your irrational and unpatriotic beliefs.

BEDTIME STORIES BY THOM YORKE

by David Hart

"The Happy Little Bunny"
Once there was a little bunny who had a little furry tail and a little shiny nose. But the electrodeath cloud of commerce strangled it and its foxhole was converted to a parking lot, a parking lot, a parking lot. Ample parking asphalted over bunny bones. Everyone everyone everyone get in.

"Hannah and Gunther"
Hannah and her brother Gunther lived in a happy wooden house at the end of a winding road by the forest. Chomping tree-eating machines grinding, halting, grinding the forest destroyed the trees—birches branches Branford—to make end tables and politician luncheon plates, spin spin spin. I can't feel my legs anymore.

"Whoopsie the Clumsy Dragon"
In the dragon family in the enchanted cave, there lived Mother, Father, Brother, and Whoopsie. Whoopsie tried to be like the other dragons, but

anytime he tried to help he ended up making a mess. Diplomats destroy the ozone and waiting, wailing. Crawl in the hole, leap the banshee, and eat the sunlight. Tonight, tomorrow, why bother? Another. Another. I'm a grown monkey wastechain.

"Everybody Enjoys Manners!"

When we eat, it's fun to have our manners eat with us! Wear your napkin on your lap and don't hit your sister, even if she throws peas at you. Reason your reasons, razors shave the planet clean. Blood fills the rivers, clogs the tubes. I want to die, eat your ice cream.

POPULAR CHILDREN'S FAIRY TALES REIMAGINED USING MEMBERS OF MY FAMILY

by Eric Silver

Cinderella—starring my sister-in-law as Cinderella.

Summary: After Cinderella's father dies, she decides to passive-aggressively punish her stepmother for having the indecency first to marry her father after her mother died, and then to outlive him. So she begins to clean the house, following everyone as they walk around, loudly moaning about how much she suffers because of all the housework she does and that it isn't helping her thyroid problem. Cinderella is the kinder nickname she is given for her fixation on the fireplace that no one uses, because "Obsessive Shrew-Bitch" wouldn't jive with the Disney people. On the night of the prince's ball, her fairy godmother comes and, to shut her up from complaining, buys her new clothes, gives her taxi money, etc. Cinderella goes to the ball, where the prince asks her to dance. She accepts, remarking that since she's been on her feet all day, a few more minutes won't make a difference. As they dance, she critiques the furnishings of the castle, then wonders aloud if all princes attend their balls without having shaved that day, or if it was just this particular prince. The prince politely excuses himself and starts up conversation with one of his advisers, even though it is the one with bad breath. Cinderella sits and scowls at the rest of the ball because they "don't know they have it so good," then takes a cab home before midnight because otherwise her eyes look puffy in the morning.

The Little Red Hen—starring my mother as the Little Red Hen.
Summary: The hen asks who will help her get the corn, take it to the mill, grind it, make flour, bake it, and whatever else she was saying while my father and I were trying to watch the *Twilight Zone* marathon on the Sci Fi Channel. My father tells her she's in front of the television. The Little Red Hen comes out after the eighth or ninth time Rod Serling pulls one of his clever twists where everybody is an alien, and asks who wants some bread. We grunt. She brings us the bread, but I see she threw raisins in, and I detest raisins in bread, unless it's cinnamon bread, so I say, "No thanks." She in turn gives me the typical guilt trip about how it's fine that even though she's been making the damn thing from scratch all day from a recipe she found in the *Times*, I won't even eat one slice. My father eats most of the bread and has stomach pains the rest of the night. I go a few more rounds with Rod before I pass out on the couch. In the middle of the night I wake up hungry and settle for a slice of the raisin corn bread. I will vehemently deny this in the morning, even though I am found on the couch with yellow crumbs on my shirt.

Peter Pan—starring my brother as Peter Pan.
Summary: Peter used to leave Never Never Land a bunch of times to visit the real world, but now when he comes to visit Wendy and the other orphans, he leaves increasingly upset, because they always seem to be judging his lifestyle. Whenever he comes flying in, he always picks a thunderstorm, and when John asks him why he doesn't check

the weather before he goes flying, Peter flips out on him and says he'll fly whenever he damned well pleases, and he has his own reasons. The kids don't even say anything about Peter growing up and acting like an adult instead of throwing tantrums, but Peter, perceptive as always, senses these judgments and stops going to the real world. He also informs Wendy that she has been a constant source of aggravation and pain to him, and that he will no longer tolerate her abuse. He runs into Cinderella on one of his fairy-dust binges, marries her, and goes off to Never Never Land, where they will bicker because he's off fighting pirates while she's cleaning the forest all day. Wendy, John, and Michael, who was previously trying to remain unbiased about the whole thing, think Peter is a jerk.

The Tortoise and the Hare—
starring my father and his Honda Civic as the Hare.
Summary: Both animals agree that they will meet at a Greek restaurant for dinner. They leave the house at the same time. The hare does not actually travel any faster than the tortoise, but he speeds up to brake fast at stoplights, makes wild, hairpin turns, and switches lanes, compulsively looking for the easiest flow of traffic. He also has his own special shortcut to get to the Greek restaurant that involves charging through the library parking lot at manslaughter speeds. The tortoise is trying to decide between the dolmades and a moussaka platter when the hare comes in, finishing his point to onlookers that his shortcut was really not much slower than the normal route. The hare orders a gyro, with the yogurt sauce on the side, and tells the tortoise that he'll just share the tortoise's salad with him.

FEEDBACK FROM JAMES JOYCE'S SUBMISSION OF *ULYSSES* TO HIS CREATIVE-WRITING WORKSHOP

by Teddy Wayne

Great opening hook, but do you need 96-point Garamond for the *S*? Kind of feels like you're padding the page count.

Truly felt I got to know Leopold (Poldy?). Nitpicky, logistical question: Is this really how people think?

"Snotgreen" = hyphenated.

Show how these characters process memory, language, abstractions, and the urban landscape through stream of consciousness, don't just tell us.

More commas, please.

Stephen comes off a little unsympathetic. I remember you used him in a previous story—maybe you could integrate some of that material here?

Unclear where and when this is set.

Caught some allusions to *The Odyssey*. Nice.

Proper punctuation for dialogue is double quotes, not em dashes.

Balked a bit at some of Molly's "sexier" thoughts, which read like male fantasy. You can do better than this, Jim.

Think you accidentally stapled in something from your playwriting workshop for Ch. 15.

The voice reminds me of the story "Which Is More Than I Can Say About Some People" from Lorrie Moore's *Birds of America*. Read it?

"History is a nightmare from which I am trying to awake." So true.

Everything Buck said had me LOL—hilarious character! Where do you come up with this stuff?

Kick-ass work, JJ, but way too long. Have you considered turning this into a short-short?

Noticed schematic chapter variations in literary technique, bodily organ, artistic subject, color, and symbol—really complex stuff. It's obvious you spent a while on this one.

I normally appreciate your extravagant wordsmithing, but got the sense here that you wore out the Shift + F7 keys (i.e., thesaurus). "Honorific-abilitudinitatibus"? What, are you trying to impress that girl Nora?

I think you can push the experimentation even further in your next piece. Remember last week after class, when we got trashed on Guinness and came up with the ludicrous idea of a 700-page novel that puns every few words on the name of a river? Maybe there's something to that.

Typo: last word capitalized.

PHRASES ON THE MARQUEE AT THE LOCAL STRIP CLUB TO CATER TO A MORE LITERATE CROWD

by Jonathan Shipley

AHAB, CHECK OUT OUR GREAT WHITE TAIL

THE OLD MAN AND THE SEE

CHECK OUT OUR TROLLOPS, ANTHONY

THE PRINCE AND THE PEEPER

OUR GIRLS EVEN DRIVE OSCAR WILDE

ROMEO-OH-OH AND JULIET

IT'S ULYSSES TO RESIST US

A TALE OF TWO TITTIES

OUR POETRY IN MOTION WILL HAVE E. E. CUMMING

LEAVES OF ASS

WE'RE PRETTIER THAN JOHN GREENLEAF WHITTIER

STRIPPY LONGSTOCKING

THE HOS OF KILIMANJARO

LADY MACBETH ON AMBIEN

by Laurence Hughes

Dunsinane. Anteroom in the castle.
Enter a DOCTOR OF PHYSIC and a WAITING GENTLEWOMAN.

GENTLEWOMAN

Two nights have I seen her rise from her bed, throw her nightgown upon her, and proceed in slumbery agitation to the kitchen, where she did claw through the pantry in the slobbering manner of a wild beast.

DOCTOR

'Tis passing strange, for I did minister to her with Ambien, that some call zolpidem tartrate, which vouchsafes eight hours of uninterrupted sleep—great nature's second course, chief nourisher in life's feast.

GENTLEWOMAN

She seeks other nourishment; two nights past she ate an ox. Lo you, here she comes! *(Enter Lady Macbeth wearing a lobster bib.)* This is her very guise, and, upon my life, fast asleep.

DOCTOR

What is it she does now? See how she rubs her hands, in the manner of one washing.

GENTLEWOMAN

'Tis her custom to wash before a meal.

DOCTOR

Still she rubs her hands, and smacks her lips also, as one who anticipates a prolonged graze at a smorgasbord.

GENTLEWOMAN

Zounds! With what unnatural fury does she fly at the larder! Her hands like talons do tear at the contents! See how victuals fly in all directions!

DOCTOR

With both hands she scoops up comestibles of every variety and with gusto shoves them in her cakehole!

LADY MACBETH

Num-num...num-num...

DOCTOR

Hark! She speaks. And with her mouth full, too.

GENTLEWOMAN

She doth ingest in a manner gross and vile. Thus have I known swine to feed.

DOCTOR

In sooth, her behavior is very like the swine, for mark you, she is down on all fours and squealing. What! She means to challenge the family dog for possession of the bones that are the detritus of the evening repast.

LADY MACBETH

Out, damned Spot! Out, I say!

DOCTOR

Indeed, note how, with teeth bared, she bids the dog retire.

GENTLEWOMAN

With what vigor does she suck the marrow! Ne'er have I seen this good and noble lady tie on the feedbag so.

DOCTOR

Now does she rummage in King Duncan's private stores, and without hesitation scarf his favorite delicacy!

LADY MACBETH

Yet who would have thought the old man to have had so much blood pudding? *(She burps.)*

DOCTOR

What a belch is there! The heart is sorely burned.

GENTLEWOMAN

Methinks the lady doth ingest too much. Now are the cupboards bare, and all the food consumed; yet see how she still comes looking for seconds. She hath a lean and hungry look.

DOCTOR

Well, hungry anyway.

LADY MACBETH

Mickey D's! *(Exit.)*

GENTLEWOMAN

Haste! She makes for the castle of McDonald, the thane whose kitchen is celebrated for its tasty offerings and swift service.

DOCTOR

He whose crest bears the golden arches? But surely the household will be abed at such an hour.

GENTLEWOMAN

The drive thru is open 'til midnight. Come!

Exeunt.

ALTERNATE ENDINGS TO FAMOUS LITERARY WORKS AS WRITTEN BY A FIFTEEN-YEAR-OLD WITH A GRUDGE

by Paul Krumholz

"Rip Van Winkle," by Washington Irving

After retreating to the woods on a hunting trip, Rip Van Winkle drinks a mysterious potion and falls asleep for twenty years, during which the American Revolution passes him by. When he awakens, he finds that his friend Dan, who can be a real asshole sometimes, has written "Balls" on his forehead. Then Dan tells everyone at school about it.

The Odyssey, by Homer

This is the tale of a Greek warrior, Odysseus, and his journey from Troy back to his homeland of Ithaca, where he left his wife and family during the ten-year expedition. Except, when Odysseus arrives back, he finds that one of his friends (ha!—more like one of his *ex*-friends, Dan!) made out with his wife, Stacey McLellan, at a party over the weekend, even though his friend knew how much Odysseus really liked her.

The Invisible Man, by H. G. Wells

A mysterious scientist named Griffin discovers a chemical formula to turn the human body invisible, but is dismayed to find that he is permanently stuck in his invisible state. He then goes over to the high school and just sits in the girls' locker room for, like, five hours and probably sees Dan's older sister showering.

Oedipus Rex, by Sophocles

Oedipus, after being cast out of his hometown of Thebes in ancient Greece due to a fateful prophecy proclaiming that he would kill his father and marry his mother—the king and queen of Thebes—is adopted by the king and queen of Corinth, whom he assumes to be his true parents. However, after hearing the prophecy, Oedipus leaves Corinth and the king and queen, whom he believes the prophecy is about, in order to protect them. On his expedition, though, he does unknowingly encounter and murder his true father, and later he marries his mother, who bears his children. Upon realizing his real parents' identities, Oedipus stabs himself in the eyes with needles to blind himself forevermore from his sins, proclaiming, "Why couldn't it have been my friend Dan's mom? She's such a MILF!" Yeah, I went there, Dan.

THE EARLIER EPIC BATTLES
OF GRENDEL'S MOTHER

by Eric Silver

Grendel's Mother vs. the Manager at ShopRite

When Grendel's mother tries to buy twenty-four cans of tuna using her "Buy five, get the sixth free" coupon, the cashier informs her that the coupons are limited to one per visit. Grendel's mother rips the cashier's throat out and asks to see the manager. After weeks of grappling and much bloodshed, the manager concedes that Grendel's mother can use four coupons in this visit. Grendel's mother hands the manager his severed leg and apologizes for the confusion.

Grendel's Mother vs. Grendel's Seventh-Grade Teacher

Enraged that Grendel will not be placed in honors math, Grendel's mother has a parent-teacher conference with Mr. Isman.

MR. ISMAN
While Grendel is quite a bright young, um, pupil, we just don't have enough room in the honors class for him, and we believe he will be adequately served by the standard seventh-grade track.

GRENDEL'S MOTHER
Braaak! Gnarsh!

She then explains that she will grasp one of the other students in the manner of a cudgel and start swinging, bludgeoning to death as many students as it takes until room opens up for her son. Mr. Isman requests a larger classroom.

Grendel's Mother vs. Grendel
Grendel, on winter break, returns from college with his new girlfriend, a human girl, Joyceline, from the surface, who is majoring in psychology. Grendel's mother sits sullenly at the kitchen table, hardly making conversation.

JOYCELINE
It must have been hard raising Grendel as a single mother, but you did such a great job.

GRENDEL'S MOTHER
Hmm? Oh, gnarsh.

Grendel excuses himself after dinner to help his mother with the dishes in the kitchen of her underwater lair, then asks her what the problem is. Grendel's mother complains that Joyceline is not mereish and that she won't take their relationship seriously, since Grendel obviously isn't looking to marry this girl. Grendel protests, but G.M.

starts badgering him, asking how he's going to bring up the children, assuming they'll swim down to her lair to visit only once or twice a year. The two argue, break dishes, and gnash their teeth at each other for a while, finally agreeing to disagree. Tensions are still running high when they return to the dinner table and try to enjoy the baklava, which got waterlogged on the trip down. Weeks later, Grendel tells Joyceline he doesn't think it will work out.

Grendel's Mother vs. Tom Cruise

Grendel's mother, an avid Oprah fan, is initially concerned about her longtime celebrity crush, Tom Cruise, when she sees his now-famous appearance on Oprah's show. His engagement to Katie Holmes only exacerbates the situation, as G.M. is painfully reminded of Grendel's father disappearing one night after going to the store for a six-pack of grog, then reappearing ten years later with a younger wife, demanding visiting rights. Tom's comments on postpartum depression, however, send her over the edge. She remembers the months after giving birth to Grendel, and how she found herself overwhelmed at home. She had trouble sleeping, yet often felt tired. Some days she felt like she had lost something that she would never get back. In the middle of devouring a man's intestines, she would just walk away, unheeding of the man's pained screams. One Sunday, before her weekly battle with the *Times* crossword, she sits down and writes an incensed letter to Cruise, proposing that instead of talking at each other they actually sit down and discuss the issue like two adults, or at least meet and battle until one of them has been sufficiently mauled and beaten to death. Cruise replies with a form letter thanking her for her support, and a signed headshot.

POUND-ELIOT SESTINA

by Alfred Corn

T. S. Eliot never wrote a sestina.
I guess he was afraid of copying Pound;
Or else doubted his metrical finesse. If
We rate poets according to form, he blew.
With Old Possum, it's like free verse all the way.
Yet, except for "Sestina: Altaforte"

And "Mauberly," form wasn't Ez's forte,
Either, assuming that means the sestina,
The villanelle, the sonnet. Yet there's a way
To give the term a wider relevance. Pound
On the podium, rave, fume until you're blue
In the face, but free verse is here to stay. If

They want an audience—this is a huge "if"—
Poets should know most readers under forty
Loathe rhyme and *ta-dum, ta-dum, ta-dum.* Joe Blow
Knows zip about the sonnet or sestina.
He buys Bukowski paperbacks by the pound.
Would he groove on Gioia or Hacker? No way.

"Little Miss Muffet, eating her curds and whey"—
Form is all just Mother Goose to Joe B. If
Asked, he'd probably say he didn't like Pound
Or Eliot so much, either. Meanwhile, for T.
S. E. (whose friends called him Tsetse) "Sestina:
Altaforte" may well have plotzed. Many blue-

Bloods prefer jazz to "high culture." *Kind of Blue*
In their book's better than "Gerontion." Weigh
The two. Secondhand emotion, says Tina
Turner, is boring. So which is the real riff?
Do you like your faves *piano* or *forte*?
Is U.S. currency the dollar or pound?

Both, from time to time, paid bills for Ezra Pound,
Our poet-chameleon. Winds of change blew
Where they would, and he followed, "Altaforte"
Is just *one* approach he took. I mean, it's way
Too hard for most bards to get down with. Me, if
I had to write villanelles and sestinas

Every week, I'd blow my brains out. Sestinas
Rock, sure, but they're not my forte. Write as if
I were those guys? There must be another way.

THE PHILADELPHIA FLYERS HAVE A TIME MACHINE: MARY SHELLEY

by Dave Johnston

Chris Therien, former Philadelphia Flyer defenseman and on-ice liability, stood outside a small English farmhouse as the first strong winds of a storm blew through the night sky. As lightning began to crack and thunder rumbled nearby, he knocked on the door. The Philadelphia Flyers had lent him their time machine so he could take on odd jobs. Therien had recently branched out to babysitting, having tired of raking leaves.

The door of the farmhouse let out a long, groaning creak as it was opened, and there stood a small girl. A small girl who shrieked at the sight of six-foot-five-inch Therien, as soon as she realized that the darkness that encompassed the entire doorway was a person.

"Mary Shelby?" Therien asked, which caused the little girl to stop screaming and stare blankly up at him. Therien looked at the words scratched into his palm by a ballpoint pen.

"I'm sorry—Shelley."

The little girl's fingers curled up as she began to scream again.

"What's the matter?" Therien asked, lurching into the Shelley house. His shoulders bashed against the doorjamb, causing the building to shudder. Therien, with the flexibility of a hard pretzel, raised his arm to little Mary Shelley and patted her head gently, which nearly knocked her out. "I brought Jenga."

Mary turned and scampered up the stairs on her hands and feet.

"Okay, you hide, I'll seek," Therien said as he began to wander up the stairs, each step cracking the plaster walls of the tiny house and making the foundation groan.

"Are you in...here?" Therien asked as he accidentally shoved his hand through the door to Mary's parents' bedroom. They had gone out for the night to do whatever nineteenth-century people did, which probably involved being amazed by gunpowder or participating in a stoning. It was Mary Shelley's father, a heavy drinker, who had hired Chris Therien.

Therien peeked into Mary's bedroom, which was simply appointed with a dresser and a small bed. Propped up against the pillow was a small blonde porcelain doll that strongly resembled little Mary Shelley. Enchanted, Chris Therien picked it up.

"Pretty," he whispered as he accidentally ripped off and then crushed the doll's head. He turned to see a silent Mary Shelley standing in the doorway. Stunned, she turned and ran.

Chris Therien followed and found her curled up in the family's bathtub.

"Is it bath time?" Therien asked, unsure if he should charge more for bathing children.

Mary screeched, the sonic power of the sound cracking the thin panes of glass in the bathroom.

"How about we have some popcorn and watch *The Goonies*?" Therien asked, completely unaware that the early nineteenth century had neither microwave ovens nor DVD players.

Mary, finding courage, shook her head petulantly.

"No, huh? Oh, I forgot to tell you—I brought a friend," Therien said, with an exaggerated wink.

Little Mary Shelley's eyes widened in terror.

"The TICKLE MONSTER!" Therien yelled, reaching toward the suddenly pale child, who ducked his advance and ran through his legs. Therien's problem was that he attempted to look through his legs, something he hadn't been able to do since third grade.

Third grade was also the last time he did a somersault, which was what he did now, into the bathtub, crushing it just as he'd crushed the doll's head.

"Arrr-irrr!" roared Therien as he struggled to get to his feet and, with both arms stuck straight out, roamed mindlessly through the small bathroom, knocking down tinctures, balms, liniments, and salves. Which was quite reminiscent of his performance in the 2002 National Hockey League play-offs.

"Stop it!" yelled Mary Shelley from the safety of the hallway.

"Arrr-irrr!" continued Therien as he jumped up awkwardly, slammed his head into the doorjamb, and pinballed back toward the breakable parts of the bathroom. Slipping on an ointment, he collapsed on the floor, howling.

"What's wrong?" Mary Shelley asked carefully.

Chris Therien held up his massive hand and, tears welling in his dull, lifeless eyes, pointed to a small sliver of porcelain embedded in his palm.

"It's just a splinter," Mary said. "I can get it out."

And with her tiny English girl hands, she quite easily got the splinter out of the behemoth's hand. She watched one final tear of gratitude roll down his face.

"Mmmmm." Therien made a yummy noise as he stroked Mary's face heavily with his hand. She sat down on the floor next to him and patted his back. "You know, I've never babysat before," Therien confessed as he absentmindedly licked his hand.

"Really?" Mary asked politely, picking up her parents' shattered toiletries.

"You know what people have always told me? That I'm a trier, not a doer," pouted Therien. "That and 'Next time remember your skates.'"

"You haven't been the worst babysitter I've ever had," Mary said, trying to cheer up the man who for many years was usually directly responsible for most of the goals scored against the Flyers.

"I know what'll make us feel better—let's make s'mores!" he exclaimed.

Buoyed by Mary Shelley's praise, he rocketed to his feet, slamming his head into an oil-filled lantern hanging from the wall and knocking its fiery contents to the floor.

"Quick, get the sand bucket," Mary yelled as the flames spread rapidly.

"No, fire hates water. I know exactly what to do," Therien countered. He grabbed Mary's hand and pulled her out of the bathroom.

Minutes later, Mary watched as her family's home, defying the first drops of a rainstorm, burned to the ground while Therien tried to call 911, not cognizant of the fact that the nearest cellular tower was a couple hundred years away.

"It's still ringing," he told her, his hand over the phone.

Mary's neighbors, intrigued by the flames shooting hundreds of feet in the air, ran up carrying torches and pitchforks, as they were wont to do.

"What 'appened 'ere?" demanded a man with a charming Cockney accent and a jaunty cap.

"Fire," Therien said as one lone tear ran down the front of his monstrously blocky head. "Bad."

JOHNSON'S LIFE OF BOSWELL

by Teddy Wayne

Nov. 17, 1764.

Boswell persists in tracking my every Movement. I have not yet detected his Motive, but he often beseeches me to "say something memorably wise and pithy," or "discourse on the Immorality of your fellow Man." When I do, or even refrain and tell him I'm too fatigued, he scratches down Notes on a Parchment. To-day I looked up from my Broadsheet whilst sipping a Mug of Ale in the *Spotted Pig* to find him at the End of the Table, observing me as a Scientist does his Microscopic Specimen. We made Contact of the Eyes and he furiously scribbled something before departing with Alacrity. Can you pronounce the Adjective "bizarre"?

Dec. 2, 1764.

At first the Attention was flattering, but now it is verging on pathetick; *Boswell* seems to have no Life other than documenting mine. The other Day I asked him if he would not prefer to follow around some attractive aristocratick Lady closer to his own Age, and he replied, with an Expression of utter Sobriety, "Why pursue the Capricious Follies of our Age when I have an Eternal Soul in you?" Then he asked for my Thoughts on Petticoats as a Symbol of engulfing Vanity.

Dec. 19, 1764.

We were picking Names out of a tricornered Hat at the *Spotted Pig* for the traditional Clandestine Gift-Exchange. Unfortunate Event, Number the First: I picked *Boswell.* Unfortunate Event, Number the Second: *Boswell* frowned when he read the Name he had picked, then entreated *Oliver Goldsmith* to switch Names with him, and once the Transaction was completed, skipped away whilst giggling to himself.

Dec. 24, 1764.

Christmas Eve at the *Spotted Pig*, and *Boswell* presents me with a Fountain-Pen carved of *African* Ivory that definitely cost more than the maximum Allowance of ten Pence. "Happy Clandestine Gift-Exchange!" he beamed. "Now your Pen shall be as liquid and infinite as your Mind as you complete *Lives of the Most Eminent English Poets*!" I had to thank him in front of everyone, then hand over my Gift. "Oh, Dr. *Johnson*, how fortuitous that we are each other's Clandestine Gift-Exchangers!" he shouted so everyone could hear. "It is as if Destiny itself had a Hand in the Selection!" When he opened his Present—a Parchment requesting he physically restrain himself from drawing within two Furlongs of me—he howled, "I *love* Gifts that play Gags on the Recipient!" and slapped me much too hard on the Back.

Dec. 25, 1764.

A quiet *Christmas* at Home, savouring *Virgil* in front of my Hearth, when I heard a Knock at my Door. I wish there were some Way of identifying who was calling before I opened the Door, because there stood *Boswell*, with a Pot of Stew and a Smile across his Face as if he were consuming Excrement and thoroughly enjoying it. We had absolutely *nothing* to talk about, but we did so nonetheless for five Interminable Hours.

Jan. 1, 1765.

Here is a Riddle: What is prying, parasitick, and makes a Perfect Ass of himself at your *New Year's* Party? The Answer on all three Accounts is, irrefutably, *Boswell*! After he arrived uninvited (under the Pretense that his Friend "John, whose family Name I cannot recall," told him to come) and had a few Goblets, he paraded around with a Candelabrum atop his Head whilst singing bawdy Songs from *The Beggar's Opera*. I saw him buttonholing *Edmund Burke* at the End of the Night—poor Man. When he asked me if he could "partake of my Sofa for the Remainder of the Evening and Morn" and I replied that "a Man of Prudence takes neither Compliments nor House-Guests without Suspicion," he seemed just as happy as if I'd let him stay.

Jan. 7, 1765.

To-night at the *Spotted Pig* I was eating my customary *Sunday* Supper when I espied *Boswell* entering. I groaned, thinking my Meal ruined, but he merely extended his Greetings to me and went off to converse with *Burke* at his Table. Have I finally rid myself of this noxious Pest?

Feb. 10, 1765.

It has been two Fortnights since *Boswell* last talked to me. I saw him at the *Spotted Pig* last Week with *Burke*, and I am fairly assured he noticed me before they rapidly exited. In his Haste, he left behind a Scrap of Parchment; it read "Notes for Life of *Burke*." To-night I shall immolate it in my Hearth.

Feb. 14, 1765.

Valentine's Day. Alone. I sent him a Parchment with several new Witticisms and Axioms of mine two Days ago, but have received no Reply. Here is one I came up with to-day: *One is not aware of what one possessed until the Moment that which was formerly possessed has become absent.* Oh, but when did my treasured Fountain-Pen start inking such stilted Prose? I need to forget about him. Perhaps find another Biographer. But where—the *Spotted Pig?* No Biographers of his Calibre spend their Time there. Stop—this is Weakness and Fear speaking; first I must be contented with myself, in Solitude, before I meet another Biographer. I must acclimate to my Life without *Boswell.*

IKEA PRODUCT OR LORD OF THE RINGS CHARACTER?

by Caley Feldman

1. Faramir
2. Freden
3. Grundtal
4. Boromir
5. Molger
6. Galdor
7. Freda
8. Agerum
9. Babord
10. Frodo
11. Griima
12. Akurum
13. Brunkrissla
14. Sultan Högbo

Lord of the Rings characters: 1, 4, 6, 7, 10, 11. IKEA products: 2, 3, 5, 8, 9, 12, 13, 14.

THE AMERICAN CANON OF THE CHOOSE-YOUR-OWN-ADVENTURE

by Matthew Collison and Chris McCoy

A Selection from the Posthumously Published Ernest Hemingway Choose-Your-Own-Adventure, *A Very Short Death*, c. 1959

It was late summer and you were alone in the café. You were sipping vermouth and reading about the war. You liked the way the vermouth tasted good when you drank it with your mouth. The war was going badly.

You tapped your tired fingers on the arm of the wooden chair where you were sitting in the café when it was dark and late. You liked how the chair was made of wood.

"Oh darling, you mustn't talk such rot," she had said.

"I'll kill him."

You felt broken and drunk in the cool night and remembered the white boat on the river.

DID YOU?

a. Grit teeth and think about the war.

b. Order a brandy that overflowed and ran down the stem of the glass and think about the war.

c. Notice the electric light hanging over the empty terrace and think about the war.

A Selection from the Unfortunately Abandoned William Faulkner Choose-Your-Own-Adventure, *The Lost and the Vanquished*, c. 1931

"Yessum," Anna had said, in that time where she felt like a very young woman, having only just realized she had come from what might be called a race, what the Lord's law required her to call a family.

Papa was smoking his blind hard pipe on the ancient porch, humming a song mother had taught him. Summer after summer, the uncertain house built without nails had remained solid as rock, rigidly guarding the county lines like a single, bleached sentinel, sending its ponderable silhouette to the furthest rung of the Alabama earth; sulking, mewing, judicate of time, wellspring and end of grace.

"Think of the folks down the hill," Papa said. Ellie was broken up in the barn crying about the negro who had broken his leg twisted under Papa's plow.

DID YOU?

a. Cough silently in the sheen of the brightly burning Lamb.

b. Cut your thumb on Stuart's knife.

A Selection from the Long-Suppressed Henry Miller Choose-Your-Own-Adventure, *Moloch-Exus*, c. 1934

You stand on the second hand of a clock and ravage the next thousand years. The entire world crumbles in front of your big prick, the dawn breaking on a broken world of your creation, and you send up a prayer demanding more light.

In the window across from you, a woman stands knock-kneed with her cunt pushed forward, holding the edge of her dress with greasy fists. Marvelous if she were to suddenly fall through the glass! Dream of the men bleeding from their feet on the sidewalk below, their frock coats dragging through the splinters!

You have found God in His burning bush and have risen from the ashes beneath its branches. You are in a sore struggle with the French girl, but it isn't possible for you to last with her crying and her mumbling: *oh, c'est bon!*

You think about how the stars have exploded, and the birds that came from the death of the heavens are not as free as you.

DO YOU?
a. Swallow the confusion which nourishes the artist and makes him madly inhuman, and come.
b. Come, and stare at your crumpled pants.

A Selection from the Recently Discovered Jack Kerouac Choose-Your-Own-Adventure, *Bop Affirmation*, c. 1955

You're trudging in the riverbottom sand when *zoooom*, there goes a flatbed truck and you're suddenly on the back of the truck with two Nebraska farm boys and you're weeping, "Y-e-e-e-e-e-s," yes to the blue swing swing of the Bird, yes to Charlie Parker, that shimmering saxophone, yes to the original mind, yes to this uncompromising romp through the heartland, you who labored on the railroad with crimson sun on your back, you who know the *palabra*, you who look right into the blowin' breeze and cry and moan and shout

AND...
a. Discover a rainbow.
b. Go off to pick oranges with the Mexican girl.
c. Sing in a rising crescendo, "Y-e-e-e-e-e-e-e-s."

POSTCARDS FROM JAMES JOYCE
TO HIS BROTHER STAN

by Martin Dibl

February 14, 1907
Dear Stan

I'm in Rome now. Still blind, of course. Listened to Nora describe the ceiling of the Sistine Chapel to me. "Ooh," she says, "doesn't Moses have big hands!" Good Lord.

Jim

June 4, 1920
Dear Stan

News from Paris. In addition to being blind I now get migraine headaches. They're so painful I have to stop working so I can scream in pain for about three hours. I'm a big hit with the neighbors.

JJ

March 10, 1922
Stan—

Met some fat American today. Wants to be a writer. Wants to take me hunting. Put his gun in my hands. At least, I think it was his gun.

   J
P.S. Still blind.

September 25, 1936
Stan—

Got a caraway seed stuck in my teeth at lunch today. It's really killing me. Been trying everything to dislodge it all day. Tongue, floss, toothpicks, table knives. It's really making me crazy.

   Jim
P.S. Hey, I got it out!

February 27, 1923
Stan—

Figured out what the next book is about. Takes place in America and there's this guy who takes pictures of bridges. He falls in love with a farmer's wife or something.

   Either that or it's a book about a guy who hates ham. Haven't decided yet.

   J

March 25, 1937
Stan—

Just found my pencil. Been looking for it all morning. Things are definitely looking up...

   J

August 26, 1928
Stan—

Hired a new secretary named Beckett. Writes letters for me. I read them and I have no idea what he's talking about. One to the phone company starts, "The bill. The bill. The bill. I can't talk about the bill." What the hell does that mean? It means I am in hell.

   jj

December 17, 1931
Stan

Greetings from Paris. Yesterday, my son said, "Let's go see Napoleon's tomb." Yes, let's, I thought. And don't let the fact that I'm blind stop us. Christ.

   And even if I could see, why would I want to look at the remains of a dead Corsican when there are hookers flashing their hoo-hahs in Pigalle? Idiots.

   J

June 16, 1940
Stan

Summer is here. Remember when we were kids, all the fun we used to have running through the fields, swimming in the river, and laughing our heads off? And then, before we knew it, it was time for dinner and we'd ask ourselves, "Where did the day go?" Yeah, me neither.

   Jimbo

May 15, 1911
Stan

Greetings from Trieste
   People in this city don't know how to walk. Either they take little

mincing steps or long loping strides. I don't know how much longer I can stand it.

JJ

November 9, 1915
Stan

Had a wonderful dinner last night—some delicious Swiss wine, a lovely steak, and then, to top it all off, flan. Wish you could have been here.

Your flan-loving brother, James
P.S. How's life in the internment camp?

August 20, 1932
Stan

Yesterday my daughter asked me if I would run off and join the circus with her. Isn't that precious? She said the two of us could do a high-wire act together and be famous all over Europe. "The Flying Joyces," she called us. Ah, the joys of fatherhood. I only wish she wasn't twenty-five.

Jim

February 2, 1938
Stan

So I wake up this morning and suddenly I can see. Good news, right? Wrong. My agent tells me that the "blind writer angle" is key to our sales. So whenever anyone comes over, I have to put on the dark glasses, carry a cane, and bump into shit. Somebody shoot me.

J

January 11, 1941
Dear Asshole

You still owe me fifteen pounds from lunch last month, and when I get out of hospital next week I'm gonna come over there and kick you until you're dead.

    Your brother, Jim

PORTRAIT OF THE ARTIST AS A MIDDLE-AGED TOEFL TEACHER

by Rob Curran

The pocket watch on the desk says nine o'clock in the Pre-intermediate Level Berlitz English Class, Trieste, Austria, October 15, 1919. On the blackboard: "Grammar Point: There is/There are (revision). Vocabulary: City buildings." James Joyce sits on the desk wearing round glasses and a jacket with tails. Of the fifteen chairs around him, only three have occupants.

JAMES JOYCE

... so the English language fills our days and works ... Weekends good?

ROMANO

Er, Tuesday.

JOYCE

What a wonderful connection to make. Your weekend has spilled right into today, Tuesday, I love it.

ROMANO

Oh, haha, I thought you say what day? It is raining heavily, no?

JOYCE

Weekend, Tuesday, raining, you are flowing my friend, let your mind continue and you will soon be sitting at the feet of Socrates. Brilliant. How about you, Stefan, did you have a good weekend?

STEFAN *{speaking from the tonsils}*

I eated the cheese. This fondue. Father bringed the Swiss friends to visit new bank.

JOYCE

Perfect. Why not cling onto your Germanic diction, Stefan? You likely exist on food your servile, farm-animal ancestors produced but had no part in naming, leaving you powerless to claim the Latinate languages as your own. Better continue with your bovine noises, making those incomprehensible sounds that are yours by heritage, yours by right. Your family's past is the steaming trail of silage leading to your mind, as marginalized as a cow's arse, and now you fart out that noxious English as a symbol. Nicely done. Molly, good weekend?

MOLLY

I went to the circus and sat in a wet seat that made my bum itchy a man must have noticed me scratching because he leant over and...

JOYCE

We're going to have to work on your breathing, Molly, but I love your language. I also love circuses. Roll up, roll up, for today we will attempt the most death-defying, grammar-rectifying, sensational exercise in sniffing memory.

STEFAN

What page?

JOYCE

Page, no page, there is no book. There are no books. Are there any blocked noses here? No, well there is nothing else I need to know. We are each going to choose a city and describe the place by using its distinctive smell.

ROMANO

What is this esmell?

JOYCE

Let me give you an example. Take a city like, let's say, well, let me think, let's say, Dublin.

ROMANO

Dubrovnik?

JOYCE

Dublin, Ireland. In Dublin the smell of hops burning in the Guinness factory grows legs & the toasted air skips over the seams of the footpath-slabs in Westmoreland Street; it crosses the Gresham Hotel's cellar-grate and the beer barrels thunder;

STEFAN

Can we do exercise in book? I don't understand usage of "There is/There are" in the uncountable noun.

JOYCE

the toasted air waits for the tram with a chattering matinee crowd outside the Ambassador Theatre; it tickles the nose of Parnell's statue on the square; it teases the gurrier on Gardiner Street who mistakes it for his mother's cooking; it finds a lost seagull crying on the North Circular Road;

STEFAN

Other teacher says that uncountable noun has "there are."

JOYCE

the toasted air altercates with the Rotten-egg Smell of the Liffey about which pub to visit; the Smell of the Liffey favors the cheap pints in Fibbers; the toasted air points out that Doyles serves late pints; the Smell of the Liffey stomps ahead of the toasted air and moans all the way up O'Connell Street; as a compromise the toasted air & the Rotten-egg Smell of the Liffey waft arm-in-arm into The Flowing Tide on Abbey Street where the disconsolate barman keeps them waiting upstairs even though they are the only ones at the bar apart from the Compost Smell of Spilt Beer.

STEFAN

"There is/there are"?

JOYCE

I was saving that for the epiphany. There are seagulls shitting now all over the pillars at the General Post Office and at the Bank of Ireland, there are seagulls shitting on the oily skin of the Liffey & there are seagulls shitting on all the workers loading hops into all the furnaces inside the Guinness factory walls. All right, Molly, what city's smell can you tell us about?

MOLLY

.... in Trieste the canal is chocolate with the white ice cream mountains you can see sometimes not since the fog came down I cannot walk in the evenings I go to the circus...

JOYCE

Breathe, girl, breathe. Excellent. Exactly what I was going for. You didn't use the grammar point of course, or the vocabulary point, or, technically speaking, your sense of smell. Excellent, nevertheless. Anyone else?

STEFAN *{sighs}*

In Zurich, there is one town hall, there are some kirches, there is one police headquarters.

JOYCE

I've never thought of "town hall" as an odor, but now I imagine I'll smell it everywhere I go. Wonderful work, your fractured grammar communicates the misery of existence in Zurich perfectly. Romano?

ROMANO

Er, Tuesday?

OUR TOWN APOLOGIZES

by Matthew Simmons

STAGE MANAGER

You no doubt remember Grover's Corners, New Hampshire. Nice, quiet town, unfamiliar with the gaze of public scrutiny. At one time, perhaps, but no more.

I have been asked by the city fathers, in my capacity as spokesman and conscience of our little town, to offer an apology from the citizens of Grover's Corners to you for our recent scandalous behavior. Like many small-town folks, we in Grover's Corners care very deeply about the war effort. And it was that effort we believed we were assisting when we fell for the smooth talk of a traveling salesman.

Over here is our Town Hall, and this is where the stranger, while he spoke honeyed words of our patriotic duties, brought an assortment of calendars out of his suitcase. Each was created in a small town like our own and featured, each month, a tasteful photograph of one or more citizens of that town in the buff. Naturally, we were shocked. Had these people lost their senses? No, the stranger assured us. Each town had produced the calendars—with his help—in an effort to raise charitable donations. The people of Deerfield, for example, had let themselves be photographed in their natural states to battle the influenza. Rochester had set its sights on rickets. And we, the stranger told us, would be participating in a furtherance of the war effort. Well, the phrase "the war effort" is a siren's song to the good people of Grover's Corners. After far too swift and far too polite a debate, we agreed to the stranger's terms, and the messy business began.

This is Elm Street. Yonder is the home of the widow Foster, and out back is her garden. There she stood, naked as the day she was born, for the camera of that wandering salesman, next to the heliotrope she tends to year in and year out. Old Mr. Foster loved that heliotrope, and he loved the naked bosom of his dearest Barbara, that day exposed to a gentle breeze and a gathered crowd of children.

Over here on Main Street is the bank. Up there is the window of the office of the banker Cartwright, the richest man in town. He was also the only man brave enough to go full frontal nude, on the condition he be given the privilege of the month of January. The first month, he believed, befitted a man of his stature. His "stature" turned out to be less than impressive, though, standing in his home before a roaring fire in nothing but his socks and garters.

Here's the Presbyterian Church. The Protestants took more readily to the calendar than the Catholics. The tenor section of the choir posed in a sort of boudoir setting, stretched on velvet couches, draped in gauzy veils. Who knew Grover's Corners had such things? Who knew the Presbyterians had such things? The Methodists, maybe. But there you are. Lives you would never guess at are lived behind closed doors. The choir was April, the month of rebirth.

And right here's a big butternut tree.

You remember Rebecca Gibbs. Here in the Gibbs's home, she lost much more than her youth to the traveling salesman. He was a charmer. A young girl of eighteen she was at the time, and had a sweetheart in France. No more, though. The sweetheart hasn't been back to Grover's Corners since the end of the Great War. Rebecca works at Morgan's now, serving up ice-cream sodas. Her month was August. We burned the calendars in huge bonfires, but few were thrown in with that month intact. Many a wife and mother in our town have searched in dresser drawers and under beds, but have not found where the men and boys stashed Miss Gibbs.

We're sorry. We hope this apology squares us with you and with the Office of Postal Inspection. The stranger's charity was, of course, false, and when he skipped town with the negatives, he took our innocence with him.

We ask for an end to the editorials and jokes. We are not, as one wag remarked, a "nudist colony waiting to happen." We're just a small, naive town.

Well, here comes Constable Warren on his rounds. Good night.

SHAKESPEARE'S INTERROGATORIES, OR WHY HE WANTED TO KILL ALL THE LAWYERS

by Mike Warner and Michael Pardo

RESTRAINT OF TRADE

Shylock v. Antonio

Plaintiff's First Interrogatories

Interrogatory No. 4: If you prick us, do we not bleed? If you tickle us, do we not laugh? If you poison us, do we not die? And if you wrong us, shall we not revenge?

Answer: Defendant objects to Interrogatory No. 4 on the ground that whether pricking, tickling, poisoning, or wronging is the proximate cause of bleeding, laughing, death, or the seeking of revenge, respectively, can be established only through expert testimony. Because Plaintiff has failed to timely disclose expert(s) and submit expert reports covering these subjects pursuant to Federal Rule of Civil Procedure 26, Plaintiff should be barred from presenting evidence on these points, and Defendant has no obligation to respond to this interrogatory. Subject to and without waiving this objection, Defendant denies that he pricked, tickled, poisoned or in any way wronged Plaintiff. Defendant further states that it has not yet determined who, if anyone, it intends to use as expert witnesses, but reserves the right to designate expert(s) in accordance with Rule 26.

CIVIL RIGHTS/WRONGFUL DEATH
Estate of Julius Caesar v. Cassius, Casca, Brutus, et al.

Interrogatory No. 14: Et tu, Brute?

Answer: Defendant Brutus objects to Interrogatory No. 14 on the ground that it is vague and ambiguous. Furthermore, to the extent that the interrogatory seeks to establish the actions of defendant Brutus as a proximate cause of Caesar's death, defendant asserts that the interrogatory is beyond the scope of interrogatories and is a question of fact to be determined by jury.

SANITY TRIAL
Hamlet v. Hamlet

Interrogatory No. 1: To be, or not to be: that is the question: Whether 'tis nobler in the mind to suffer the slings and arrows of outrageous fortune, or to take arms against a sea of troubles, and by opposing end them?

Answer: Defendant objects to Interrogatory No. 1 on the ground that it is overly broad, unduly burdensome, and not reasonably calculated to lead to the discovery of admissible evidence to the extent it seeks to answer one of life's unanswerable metaphysical questions. Defendant further objects on the ground that Int. No. 1 is too vague and ambiguous to permit a meaningful response due to the variation in the type of slings and arrows, and the unknown skill with which outrageous fortune may wield such.

INTENTIONAL INFLICTION OF EMOTIONAL DISTRESS
Capulet v. Montague

Interrogatory No. 4: O Romeo, Romeo! Wherefore art thou, Romeo?

Answer: Defendant objects. Defendant, in his Answer to Plaintiff's First Amended Complaint, has already conceded the court has in personam jurisdiction over him, and he has also availed himself of the Verona courts in filing his Counterclaim and Third-Party Counterclaim (see also interrogatories attached below). Any further information regarding Defendant's location is therefore irrelevant. What is more, Plaintiff and the court are aware that one of Defendant's allegations in his Third-Party Counterclaim lawsuit is that members of Plaintiff's family have threatened his life and intend to do him bodily harm with swords. Defendant considers efforts, such as this question, to ascertain his whereabouts to be related to the illegal purpose of causing him bodily harm, rather than for any legitimate purposes relating to this (or Defendant's) lawsuit. Accordingly, Defendant will seek sanctions against Plaintiff's attorneys for any further abuses of the discovery process.

VARIOUS INTENTIONAL TORTS
Montague v. Capulet, et al.

Interrogatory No. 25: But, soft! What light through yonder window breaks?

Answer: The referred-to light is a product of Star-Crossed Industries, Ltd., a division of The Capulet Co., Inc. More specifically, the no-glare, artificial light was generated by the new Star-Crossed Home Artificial Kerosene Emission System™, patent pending; the low-energy light produced is soft on the eyes and perfect for reading or any other home activity. Defendant objects to disclosing more detailed information about the light—any other information would be relevant to neither the Counterclaim nor the Third-Party Counterclaim, and, more important, it would require the disclosure of protected trade secrets. Counterclaim Defendant directs Counterclaim Plaintiff to direct any further inquiries regarding the referred-to light to counsel for The Capulet Co., Inc.

FROM THE GRAD SCHOOLYARD: THE DIARRHEA SONG

by Jake Swearingen, Edward Fairchild, and Sam King

When you're analyzing Joyce
and your butthole has no choice:
Diarrhea. Diarrhea.

When you're paraphrasing Bloom
and you're stinking up the room:
Diarrhea. Diarrhea.

When you're quoting Schopenhauer
and release a dirty shower:
Diarrhea. Diarrhea.

When you're citing Marcel Proust
and you feel that doo-doo juice:
Diarrhea. Diarrhea.

When you're laughing at Voltaire
and you flood your underwear:
Diarrhea. Diarrhea.

ON THE OCCASION, GIVE OR TAKE, OF THE FIFTIETH ANNIVERSARY OF THE FIRST STAGING, IN PARIS, OF SAMUEL BECKETT'S *WAITING FOR GODOT*, A FEW REPRESENTATIVE SELECTIONS FROM THE ANNOTATED TREASURY OF *WAITING FOR GODOT* PARODIES

by Ben Greenman

Waiting for Bedpan

London, 1954. One of the earliest known parodies of Beckett's existentialist classic was penned by the venerable drama critic Arthur Bryce. Bryce's initial reviews of the play called it "frankly idiotic," "folly at interminable length," and "a blot on the escutcheon of the theatre." When this review failed to derail Beckett's play, Bryce took it upon himself to craft this parody, in which an elderly man named Sam suffers silently in his hospital bed while he waits for the orderlies, who have been "dis-ordered" by vapid modern theater, to bring him a bedpan. To Bryce's chagrin, the play ran for only ten performances; to what Bryce later confessed was his secret delight, Beckett himself took in one of those performances while visiting London. "What a prophetic work," he quipped. "I do have to go to the loo."

Waiting for McCarthy

Berkeley, California, 1968. The rock musician Frank Zappa partially funded and may have partially written this overtly polemic work, which focused on a group of young people in despair over the popularity of Richard Nixon. Vladimir and Estragon have been renamed Michael and Michelle—some critics thought that the play was lampooning the counterculture's own brand of nonconformist conformity—and the central couple spends the first half of the play topless, lounging in bed. When Lucky enters, he is carrying two cups of black coffee and a framed portrait of Tom Hayden. Pozzo, predictably, is a crude caricature of Nixon.

Waiting for Waiting for Godot

Reed College, 1974. This play grew from a real-life incident concerning theater majors waiting for the arrival of visiting professor and Beckett expert Jonathan Burkman, who had called a meeting for Monday, 9 a.m., to discuss that semester's production of *Krapp's Last Tape*. By 10, Burkman had not arrived, and one of the students proposed writing a play about his tardiness. Another student suggested that the students' actual conversation could be used as a starting point. Done.

Waiting for Good Blow

New York, 1979. Vladimir and Estragon retained their names and most of their lines in this production, which recast them as downtown hustlers and part-time band managers meeting with their drug dealer on a Manhattan street corner. The long and somewhat sadistic set of instructions delivered to Lucky by Pozzo in Act II was left untouched. All actors wore black leather jackets and sunglasses; the soundtrack, delivered faux-amateurishly from an onstage boom box, redundantly included several songs by the Ramones, including "53rd and 3rd" and "Carbona Not Glue."

Oh! He's Here!

Coeur d'Alene, Idaho, 1985. Shortly after graduating from the theater program at Columbia University, the playwright Linton Kwesi Silverstein (née David Silverstein) broke up with his girlfriend and perennial leading lady, Elaine Wofford, who had moved with him from New York. A few nights after the breakup, a drunken and despondent Silverstein penned this absurdist reduction of Beckett's play, in which Godot appears before the first curtain is raised, looks around for Vladimir and Estragon, cannot find them, and, convinced of his solitude, urinates onstage. The play also includes a chess match between Lucky and Pozzo in which the game pieces are severed human fingers that, when touched, sing snatches of disco hits such as "More, More, More" and "Knock on Wood." There was only one known performance.

Waiting for Saddam

Baghdad, 2003. After a tattered copy of the original play found its way into the hands of students at al-Mustansiriya University, they quickly cobbled together a crude political satire that owed as much to *South Park* as to Beckett. It is not known whether the play has ever been staged, but it has been posted on the Internet. Updated daily to reflect changing political realities—the most recent draft incorporates the deaths of Uday and Qusay Hussein—the evolving work has attracted the attention of an independent television producer who has already contracted with Britain's Channel 4 and America's Fox network for a reality show called *Down and Out in Baghdad Hills*, which will follow a ragtag bunch of Iraqi comedians and satirists attempting to remake post-Hussein Iraq with the power of laughter.

UNPUBLISHED CODA
TO HARPER LEE'S
TO KILL A MOCKINGBIRD

by Tim Carvell

Atticus shot the monkey when it refused to dance. Technically, it had not so much refused to dance as refused to continue dancing—it had been doing the soft shoe for four hours, and it was getting tired. It only needed a few minutes to rest. But Atticus was having one of his moods.

Atticus had long maintained that it was a sin to kill any animal whose sole purpose was to provide delight—his favorite example being the mockingbird. The rest, of course, were fair game. In the six months since he had retired from the practice of law and taken the job of zookeeper, Atticus was putting that principle into action. He had killed eight pheasants, a giraffe, two chimpanzees, six porcupines, all the reptiles, and more blue jays than you could shake a stick at. The smarter of the animals had begun to make themselves useful: the hippos had taken up scrimshaw; the ducks were practicing their madrigals; and the remaining three giraffes busied themselves with digging graves for what Atticus liked to call "my disappointments." Nobody wanted to replicate the pandas' mistake. They had a good run for a while with their comical tumbling, but didn't realize that Atticus had grown tired of their routine until it was too late—far, far too late.

Now, in a desperate effort to keep Atticus amused, the animals worked on expanding their repertoires. The prairie dogs had a new precision dance routine every Saturday night, and the rumor was that they were beginning to look into some sort of synchronized-swimming thing, but the seals and sea lions were unwilling to help. The polar bears and grizzly bears had their soccer matches, and the penguins—well, the penguins were just so fucking charming, there was no way Atticus was going to harm them. Everyone hated the penguins.

Much later—after the Incident, after the coroners and the reporters and the Humane Society had gone home—people agreed that Atticus's mistake had been opening the wood shop. It seemed innocuous enough—the kangaroos wanted to make him key chains and coasters and picture frames, or so they claimed. But who knew that such docile, big-eyed creatures had such rage in them, or even knew how to carve a shank? Who knew—until that fateful night of the talent show— that their pouches were big enough to conceal crossbows? And who knew what could happen to a kangaroo when it had lost the power to charm?

I'll never forget the last few seconds I saw Atticus—the talent show's judge, jury, and executioner—alive. He was scowling as the flamingos wobbled through an especially ill-conceived medley. He'd barely reached his thirty-ought-six when the kangaroos bounded out from the wings and struck, with fury, speed, and precision.

And then, with no one to stop them, they took down the mocking-birds, one by one.

Only later did the police find the note the kangaroos had scrawled and left in their cages. It was a crude note, terse and ungrammatical, and filled with misspellings and typos. It had, after all, been written by marsupials. But its message was simple, stark, and—the jury later agreed—undeniably compelling: Atticus, they explained, had ceased to delight them.

CORMAC McCARTHY
WRITES TO THE EDITOR
OF THE *SANTA FE NEW MEXICAN*

by John Kennan

Dear Editor,

I enjoyed reading the article on Tuesday about putting a traffic light by the interchange of Castillo and Grand streets. I aint know nothing about politics, but I seen too many cars hit too many light poles over the years. A man gets weary of it.

Just yesterday, my wife said be careful at that stop sign.

Why? I asked.

Well just a week ago the Johnsons got sideswiped by that guy who sells those turquoise stickpins in his shop on Esmeralda.

I forgot about that, I responded. And sure enough, I was careful at that stop sign. But the driver in back of me wasnt.

A truck carrying a load of lumber down from the old ancient pine forests or the newfound wrath of a somnolent god or just the terror of fading memories hit the driver square on the left side of his Volvo.

Oh shit, the driver said, just before his life escaped into an incarnadine tributary on his steering wheel.

I dont want to see that again. A traffic light is needed, and that soon. Or we will continue to inhibit our temporary souls which wait like cowed children at stop signs, as it always was before those signs crept like stalks from the Earth.

Regards,
C. McCarthy
Santa Fe

STILL KICKING:
THE VERY AUTHORIZED
BIOGRAPHY OF STEVEN SEAGAL,
VOLUME II, PP. 567–68

by Jared Bloom

p. 567

...and although he would later describe it as an "error in judgment," Steven decided to let the Dalai Lama's third call go to voice mail and continued to rock Brandi's delicate world atop the St. Louis Arch.

"This is what awesome feels like," he assured her.

Two days later, Steven received a phone call from his agent, Joe Powers, who was raving about a script he had found earlier that morning in Bruce Willis's trash. It was the story of Mason Storm, a renegade cop who emerges from a coma seven years after discovering an attempted murder plot against a Senate candidate and exacts revenge by killing people and sexing up Kelly LeBrock.

"I like it," Steven said as he slid a green-tea popsicle across his lips.

"Politics is very popular right now." And with Congress making laws in Washington at that very moment, he was absolutely right.

The only issue left to settle was the title of the film. Joe was worried that *Untitled Bruce Willis Project* was a bit misleading, and he was sure that Steven would prefer something much more ridiculous.

"What is the point of this movie, Joseph?" Steven asked. Joe's first name was actually Jodie, but Steven thought that was way too gay to say.

"Well, they're trying to kill you, Steve. And they're finding it very difficult," Powers responded.

"So, in other words, I'm hard to kill."

With that in mind, Steven meditated for a week—the kind of meditation where you focus squarely on connecting your two eyebrows—before settling on a title. His Bruce Lee notepad was filled with possibilities, including *Difficult to Beat Up*; *Seriously, Try Punching This Guy in the Face and See What Happens*; and *Howard's End*.

In the end he settled on *Sex Fighting*, but Joe, who had been on hold this whole time, informed him that this was already taken by a Linda Lovelace movie.

"How about *Hard to Kill*?" Joe said.

"Whatever."

FRANK McCOURT'S AMERICAN HISTORY CLASS: COURSE SYLLABUS

by Derrick Martin

Week 1—The Irish

Week 2—Coming to America

Week 3—Marginalizing the Irish people

Week 4—Kicking the bog mud off your boots

Week 5—Ireland

Week 6—My father the Irishman

Week 7—The Italians?! Oh, please!

Week 8—Looking back (on Ireland)

MY MEMOIRS OF MY GEISHA

by Rick Stoeckel

The day my geisha arrives on my doorstep I feel, in a word, geishariffic! At least twice a day my geisha performs this eloquent, high-risk choreographed dance for me. She jumps around, twirls, and throws herself to the floor in beautiful, exquisite movements. I tell her she can stop when I see her getting a little tired. She knows I will be disappointed if she does stop, though. I want more. She continues dancing for about an hour or so. My geisha loves to unwind from her long, hard day of entertaining me by drawing me a warm, soothing bath, adding salts, and mixing in exotic fragrances. She improvises a song about my hairy little potbelly. I've always been self-conscious about that feature on my body, but hearing it put into song makes me feel special.

Gas prices are high, and my geisha knows that! She gives me rides to work on the handlebars of her bicycle, which I have nicknamed the geishacycle. She loves it when I weave her name into objects. When she sneezes, I tell her, "Geisha you!" It sounds a little like "God bless you."

It isn't superclever, but she smiles. I can tell when she is in a good mood because she peddles faster.

"Geisha, where is my hot tea?" I scream during my lunch break. She comes running through the crowded cafeteria, hot tea in her hands. Her grace astounds me as she avoids bumping into a single one of my coworkers, spinning and prancing around them like an acrobatic deer. She spills not a drop of tea. I can't help but think what a lucky man I am to have found such a wonderful, beautiful geisha. Uh-oh! No cinnamon in this tea. "Geisha," I say, "you take this tea back right away!" She is so sweet the way she bows and apologizes profusely. I can't stay mad at her for too long.

My geisha knows that if she wants to be a part of my life, then she needs to accept that game consoles are a major passion of mine. My geisha helps me by memorizing secret codes and studying maps from strategy books. She has become a reservoir of fantastic game tips, tricks, and hints. When I beat Luigi's Mansion for the Nintendo GameCube, my geisha did a celebratory Sarugaku dance: incredibly elegant, inspiring, and dangerous.

I enjoyed her performance almost as much as the game's ending, where Mario and Luigi jump up and down once they are reunited. Tons of Japanese names scroll down the screen as the game designers are given credit. I ask my geisha if she recognizes any of the names. She giggles and begs me to please take a shower. I guess twenty-four consecutive hours of Luigi's Mansion will ripen a person. That's another wonderful thing about my geisha; she has an incredible sense of smell!

The other day, the both of us go hang out with a buddy of mine and his girlfriend. We are all having a good discussion. Suddenly, without warning, my geisha breaks into song. For twenty minutes, all attention is on her crooning. My buddy tries to intervene with a joke, but my geisha cuts him this look that seems to say, "Geisha don't think so!" She seamlessly transitions from her Japanese lullaby into an oration on the proper way to boil rice. My friends have to leave before she concludes. Too bad they missed the best part: my geisha goes into the kitchen and actually boils rice for me! Delicious!

My geisha demands that I take off my shoes before I enter the house. I have to put on slippers. It is part of her crazy geisha custom. I tell her it is an American custom that when you enter a bedroom, you have to take off all your clothes. This has had the unfortunate drawback of her never stepping foot inside my bedroom.

What is better than a geisha? Two geishas! From the moment the knock sounds and my second geisha walks through my condominium door, they are at each other's throats. I feel like I have a front-row seat to a live *Matrix* battle. There is flipping and dance-fighting. I learn that geishas do not like competition from other geishas. I learn that there can be too much of a geisha thing.

ALICE WALKER MEETS ROY G. BIV

by Laurence Hughes

I think it pisses God off if you walk by the color purple in a field somewhere and don't notice it.

He gets put out if you walk by the color red, too. Doesn't necessarily have to be in a field. Could be anywhere.

If you walk by orange? Like, at HoJo's? He gets irked. No, wait— more like nettled. He'll be peevish, I guarantee that.

Yellow, you better be like, "Oh, wow, yellow," or He'll get all cranky with you.

Don't go ignoring green, whatever you do. Man, does He get hot under the collar if you ignore green.

Blue? Choleric, I swear.

Overlook indigo and He goes right through the roof. I mean it, He'll rip the top of your head right off.

If you walk by the color violet, He goes fucking ballistic.

TALES OF EROTICA:
CHUCK NORRIS AND ME

by Brian Bieber

Everyone loves getting turned on. Everyone loves high-kicking martial-arts action.

So I'm going to recount for you the very first heavy-petting session I engaged in with my first girlfriend when I was sixteen. But because I'm not sure that this girlfriend would appreciate me sharing these events, instead of using her real name, I'm going to refer to her as action star Chuck Norris. Likewise, any personal details about my ex-girlfriend that might implicate her directly will be changed to indicate achievements earned by Mr. Norris.

For example, instead of referring to Madeline as a junior-varsity-basketball cheerleader, I will refer to her as an international karate champion. And when I say "star of TV's *Walker, Texas Ranger*" I'll really mean "supporting cast member in a 1996 high-school production of *Jesus Christ Superstar*."

Any references to sexual activities we engaged in will be disguised as martial-arts maneuvers or maybe wrestling holds. I won't say Maddie was the first girl I ever French-kissed, I'll say something to the effect of, "Chuck Norris kicked me so hard in the mouth I had to have my jaw wired shut."

When mentioning details that still embarrass me, I will go on and on with analogies that—if you really think about them—make sense, but are pretty difficult to follow. I won't sheepishly admit that even at fifteen she was more experienced than I was. I'll ask you to imagine a younger Chuck Norris, not yet a master of his art, but perhaps an intermediate student, leading one of the newer karate students in basic "block, step, kick" exercises during the warm-up time before class, while the teacher is stretching. I won't tell you that before that afternoon on my parents' couch I had kissed only one other girl—awkwardly—on the cheek, and was quickly but gently rebuffed. Instead, I'll casually share an anecdote about the time I sparred with Steven Seagal, who let me take a couple swings at him but quickly got bored and didn't even waste the energy it would take to break a few of my bones.

The thing about Chuck Norris is that he is not the least bit pretentious. He is not without moments of gracelessness—sometimes overextending a kick or putting too much of his upper body behind a punch. His form is not nearly as fun to watch as Jet Li's exhausting acrobatics, and it is not quite as pretty as the phony grace of Jean-Claude Van Damme, whose elegance belies technique that is beautiful to look at but entirely useless in a real combat situation. More than anything, Chuck Norris is effective, and he is not self-conscious. I, on the other hand, was deathly afraid of getting a hickey.

I ran into Chuck three years after we stopped fighting regularly. We were both home from our respective colleges during a holiday break. We went to a movie one night, out to coffee another. Finally, the night before I was to return to school, our mutual animosity got the best of us and a fight broke out in the guest bedroom of my parents' house, where we had been watching *Saturday Night Live.* We had both trained hard in the previous years and were eager to demonstrate the new moves we had learned. In our eagerness, of course, we disregarded technique, and the bout quickly turned into a brawl, our limbs flailing wildly, a mess. In this way, this battle was much like our first, but not nearly as sweet.

Afterward, I walked Chuck out to his car, feeling defeated. I leaned in close to the star of the box-office flop *Firewalker* and asked if he was sure that this was okay. He smiled at me tenderly, placed a hand on my cheek—a hand that had smashed pine boards and bricks, had shattered giant blocks of ice—and then he leaped into the air and delivered a devastating flying roundhouse kick to my skull.

CHAPTER TITLES FOR RACHEL CARSON'S 1962 BOOK *SILENT SPRING* THAT WERE REJECTED FOR BEING TOO ALARMIST

by Caredwen Foley

"Slow Mercury Poisoning Giving You Amnesia and Causing You to Forget Your Mortgage Payment"

"Having Your Retinas Disintegrate from Too Many UV Rays and Finding Out the Tough Way That Your Girlfriend Is a Man"

"Phosphoric Acid Seeping into the Water Supply and Destroying Your Teeth, Leading to Your Dentist Telling You You Need a Root Canal"

"Getting Fired for Distributing 'Leftist Propaganda' About the Effects of Global Warming and Losing Your Dental Coverage Just in Time for the Aforementioned Root Canal"

CELEBRITY BIOGRAPHIES WRITTEN BY A GUY WHO CANNOT DISTINGUISH FICTION FROM REALITY

by Ben Joseph

Harrison Ford

After a lackluster high-school career at Maine Township High School East, in Park Ridge, Illinois, Harrison Ford dropped out of Ripon College, in Wisconsin, and turned to intergalactic smuggling to pay his way. After a brief stint as a war hero, he turned to academia, becoming a well-known professor of archaeology, and took up one of his most beloved hobbies, Nazi killing. It was during this period that he was reunited with his father, James Bond. Although he was briefly accused (and then exonerated) of killing his wife, it came as no surprise when, in 1997, Mr. Ford was elected President James Marshall and foiled a Kazakh terrorist attack (led by Dracula, no less!) by simply asking the terrorists to get off his plane. After doing some other things no one really cares about, he started dating single female lawyer Calista Flockhart. He and Ally McBeal currently split their time between L.A. and Wyoming.

Samuel L. Jackson

In 1993, Samuel L. Jackson was eaten by a dinosaur. Then, after arguing with a dancing Vinnie Barbarino about what hamburgers were called in France, Samuel "King of Cool" Jackson was really badass for a really long time. He accomplished this by talking loudly and using lots of harsh language. In 1997, he was almost eaten by an anaconda in the rain forests of Brazil, but then I remembered that was actually Ice Cube. He was, however, eaten by a shark in 1999. Then, he was a Jedi, and although nothing ate him he was electrocuted by an old man and some extremely bad digital effects. He was almost eaten by snakes in 2006, but, luckily, since that movie was rated R, he was able to fight them off using a fair amount of violence and some extremely harsh language. Mr. Jackson is an avid golfer and, unbeknownst to most, a vegetarian.

Arnold Schwarzenegger

Arnold spent his youth developing an ungodly physique and learning to speak English with a really funny accent. Then, some things blew up. Then, he killed some people. Then, some more stuff blew up. Then, he killed some more people. Sometimes he used a sword. Then, after almost being killed by some people, he killed them, and then blew them up. Then, after being blown up by some people who were trying to kill him, he killed them by blowing them up. At some point during that, he was a robot from the future that lost its memory and went to Mars. Or something like that. However, after such a career, he did the only thing an Austrian immigrant who can barely speak English and specializes in grimacing in front of cameras for long periods of time can do—make a cameo in *Around the World in 80 Days*, starring Jackie Chan. Oh, yeah, I think he got into politics, too.

JOHN UPDIKE,
TELEVISION WRITER

by Jared Young

Newhart

Dick Loudon, growing increasingly depressed about his middling career as a writer of do-it-yourself books, purchases a Connecticut guesthouse and moves there with his emotionally distant former mistress, Joanna. But the chill New England air only serves to heighten the tension between them, and soon Dick begins an affair with Stephanie, the chambermaid. He makes love to her against a tree; his loins, too, seem armored with bark.

Joanna learns of the affair and sets out to seduce Stephanie's fiancé, Michael. On a ski trip to Vermont, drunk on brandy, the two adulterous couples make love in adjoining rooms, but in the void of uneasy silence born from their guilt, they feel no pleasure.

The series ends as Dick dreams that he stayed married to his ex-wife. But there is no pleasure to be found in her aggressive domestic possession of him. Upon waking up, Dick goes for a walk and looks down upon the lush autumn trees, recalling a long-ago summer when he drove his father's car from rural Pennsylvania to Boston. A crow struck the windshield. The memory of the bird's mindless thrashing reminds Dick of the futility of his own reflexive lust, and for the first time in his life he looks forward to the orgasmic release of death.

Friends

Ross Geller, recently divorced, yearns for his sister's best friend, self-important professional dilettante Rachel. She senses this, and takes sadistic pleasure in taunting him with her blatant flirtations. Alone with Ross in the kitchen, she asks him to examine a mole on her breast, despite his protests that his doctorate is actually in paleontology. When his hand wanders, she slaps him across the face, the loathsome weight of a thousand lubricious advances carried in the lily-pink palm of her hand.

Ross approaches Joey, his womanizing best friend, for advice. Drunk on sherry, and feeling particularly misogynistic after losing a recent acting job, Joey suggests that Ross improve his skills in cunnilingus: "Train your tongue to find that fleshy lodestone, those sweet lips peeled back like the tender skin of a blooming orchid."

On a ski trip to Vermont, Ross finds himself alone with Rachel, but his pathetic begging—his prostrate worship of her goddess's body—disgusts her. She sends him away, and, despairing, Ross drives for hours into the darkness. He eventually stops in rural Pennsylvania, where he hires a prostitute. The hooker's indifferent tenderness reminds him of his mother.

Gilligan's Island

After the S.S. *Minnow* is caught in a freak hurricane, a group of New England socialites find themselves stranded on a desert island. Mr. and Mrs. Howell, hosts of the orgiastic party for which the *Minnow* was leased, try to exercise their authority over the others but find that their wealth means nothing in this new world. To validate her flagging sense of worth, Mrs. Howell begins an affair with the lecherous Skipper, whom she secretly loathes. Her skin, at his touch, shudders like a jungle leaf bearing the staccato bombardment of tropical rain.

Elsewhere on the island, first mate Gilligan—a lapsed Catholic whose childhood in rural Pennsylvania was fraught with awkward erotic fumblings—stumbles across Ginger bathing nude in the lagoon. As he watches, his macadamia becomes a plantain, then a rippling mango, bursting with weight.

Later, on a ski trip to Vermont, the men, drunk on coconut wine, goad the women into performing a group sex act. In the morning—the scene of their transgression lit by sunlight and sobriety—the entire group is overcome by a sweeping regret that numbs their sense of hope.

They are never rescued.

EIGHT NEW ENTRIES IN
THE 2007 WRITER'S MARKET
GUIDE TO LITERARY JOURNALS

by Scott Cunningham

Adam Pollet Review: A Journal of Adam Pollet

We're looking for fresh new perspectives on me, Adam Pollet, and all the things Adam Pollet is interested in: Brazilian chicks, Sudoku, the *Times* Sunday Styles section, Duke basketball, and premium-grade cupcakes (none of that supermarket glorified-muffin shit, please).

Goat on the Railroad Tracks

Do not send us your second- or third-best poem. We want your favored son, your bright, shining diamond, your sacrificial goat on the railroad tracks of our pages.

Leave the Cannoli

We might or might not be interested in poems about clandestine Italian American business culture in northeastern New Jersey, and we may or may not want to publish those poems in a journal that might be called *Leave the Cannoli* and that we, whoever we are, may or may not be responsible for editing. Feel free to simultaneously submit, but if we decide to take your poem, we'll meet you at the docks behind the Lucky Fish Factory at 4 a.m. Come alone. With your poem.

Road Rage Review

We're looking for work that evokes the truly American feeling of being rear-ended at a busy intersection, emerging from the car like a Greek god, pulling the cocksucker from the front seat of his BMW, ripping open his pelvis, and savagely gnawing on his shrunken prostate.

So Straight!

So Straight! publishes poems about heterosexual love and loss. We want poems that evoke the backseat of a Toyota Camry, the awkward armrests at a suburban movie theater, screaming fights in the dressing room of a J.Crew outlet, text messaging, Starbucks, and John Cougar Mellencamp.

Southern Aquitane Hill Between Cottonwood Avenue and 26th Street Review

No profanity or graphic material. No sex. No children's poems. No scenes with children learning life lessons alongside other children. No nostalgic poems, nor poems that depict a dark apocalyptic future wherein humans are controlled by fascist robots (although that certainly will be the case). In general, we are not interested in poems that explain how people die in gruesome and all-too-realistic ways, nor do we want poems that hold true love in the highest regard. We do not accept rhymed, formal, free-verse, or prose poems. Response time varies according to the quality of the submission. Sixteen pages, bound with silk, and printed on the skin of a lion. Appears once every Democratic presidential administration. No simultaneous submissions, please.

Spilled Milk

We publish poetry that makes us weep. Give us dead puppies, single mothers, and peanut-butter-and-jelly sandwiches with the crusts cut off. Show us headless dolls and lonely circus workers after dark. Take us to kickball games where an overweight child is selected last, or perhaps not at all. Lock us in a bedroom. Lose us in Disney World. Make us kill ourselves, over and over.

The Stilt

The Stilt publishes all forms, styles, and genres from the immediate offspring of Wilt Chamberlain. First cousins are okay, but please, no spouses or cousins-once-removed. DNA sample required with cover letter.

IN RESPONSE TO ACCUSATIONS THAT MY MEMOIR, *I, ELLIE KEMPER*, BORROWS NUMEROUS PASSAGES FROM RIGOBERTA MENCHÚ'S MEMOIR, *I, RIGOBERTA MENCHÚ*

by Ellie Kemper

I write today to defend myself against a literary offense of the highest degree: plagiarism.

In 1983, a twenty-four-year-old Guatemalan Indian and human-rights activist named Rigoberta Menchú took part in a series of interviews with a Venezuelan-French woman whose name I cannot remember. The taped interviews were transcribed and *I, Rigoberta Menchú* was published. Menchú would later go on to receive the 1992 Nobel Peace Prize for her work on behalf of indigenous peoples. Her memoir is, quite simply, the tale of a luckless woman living under an abusive military dictatorship.

And if I might ask: Is this really so different from my own story?

> From then on, I was very depressed about life. I was afraid of life and I'd ask myself: "What will it be like when I'm older?"

This is a passage from my memoir. Several energetic critics have also found it in *I, Rigoberta Menchú*. Evidently, similar life experiences will inspire similar wordings.

"From then on" refers to the period directly following my AP U.S. History exam, on which I received a 2. I was very upset about this, because I had previously thought that I was pretty good at U.S. history and had planned to major in history or politics in college. It now seemed that the only avenues left open to me were English or sports therapy. My once sunny outlook on life took a decidedly devastating turn.

I can't remember exactly what Rigoberta Menchú is referring to in the passage, but I believe that it has something to do with seeing her brother burn to death at the *fincas*.

Next passage:

> We were going to ask for two days holiday and if they didn't give it to us we'd go and spend Christmas somewhere else. But I was incapable of disobedience. And those employers exploited my obedience.

This is the part in *I, Rigoberta Menchú* where she and her friend Candelaria first begin working as peasant maids for a Spanish landowner. In an act of defiance, Candelaria kills and plucks the chickens for the Christmas feast but then refuses to dress them. For this, they are whipped by the Spanish landowner.

In my case, junior year of college I was an unpaid intern at Christie's auction house in New York City. We only had three days off for Christmas. The other interns made a request for two more vacation days, but I was too scared to approach Bendetta (the intern coordinator). And so there I was, December 23 and December 27 at 20 Rockefeller Plaza, fetching tuna rolls and skinny cappuccinos while everyone else was sledding.

I do not find it terribly strange that we described these events in similar fashions; they are similar stories.

Next:

"A revolutionary isn't born out of something good," said my sister. "He is born out of wretchedness and bitterness. We have to fight without measuring our suffering."

I can see how this passage is misleading. It *was* my sister who said this—but it was not my biological sister. It was my Kappa Alpha Theta sister. The Mexican staff at our House wanted to deep-six Southern Strawberry from the fro-yo machine. This was unimaginable. As Kappa Alpha Theta relies heavily on the teachings of Mahatma Gandhi, our entire House staged a nonviolent bulimia strike until the matter was resolved in our favor.

A similar situation is described by Rigoberta Menchú, except that instead of a bulimia strike, Menchú and her twelve-year-old sister go into hiding in Guatemala to avoid the government-friendly death squads.

Final passage that we will examine here:

I'm still keeping my Indian identity a secret. I'm still keeping secret what I think no one should know.

Menchú and I both close our books with these words, which—I agree—is eerie. This is not surprising in Menchú's case, because throughout her book she says things like "I am a Mayan Indian."

I am sorry to spoil the ending of my memoir, but, yes, I too am an Indian (Native American). People are surprised at this since I have red, wavy hair, an abundance of freckles, and a plump, round face. None of this necessarily screams "Indian," but, believe me, it is true. My grandfather's great-grandfather was 100 percent Sioux.

I am neither a plagiarist, nor am I Irish. I am a woman with deep and emotional experiences in her past who writes about them. Although Rigoberta Menchú communicated her experience in very similar words to mine, this only serves to reinforce the notion that *ich bin ein Guatemalan Indian woman living under abusive military dictatorships*.

Human suffering is universal and timeless.

A SERIAL KILLER EXPLAINS THE DISTINCTIONS BETWEEN LITERARY TERMS

by Charlie Anders

Bildungsroman vs. Coming-of-Age Novel

I think the main difference has to do with federal sentencing guidelines. If the courts could try your protagonist as an adult for the actions he or she takes in the book, it's a bildungsroman. Otherwise, it's coming-of-age. The coming-of-age novel is vanishing as a genre, as sentencing laws make younger and younger protagonists eligible for federal prison time. These days, Huck Finn and Holden Caulfield would be sharing a cell with Popeye, the corncob rapist from Faulkner's *Sanctuary.* Also, the main character of a coming-of-age narrative might go on a killing spree as a means of testing the limits of authority. The bildungsroman's hero, by contrast, will carve up half a dozen bank tellers as a way of forming a new identity as an adult. It's totally different.

In Medias Res vs. Nonlinear Narrative

Okay, I'm going to tell you a secret. Ready? I was the Bolton Pitchforker. That was me, and the bastards never caught me. I took a couple years off between that and the more elegant forays into mutilation for which I became famous. It used to bother me that nobody understood my artistic development. And when people did talk about the pitchfork thing, they missed the significance of me twisting the pitchfork from left to right, versus from right to left, depending on the victim. I had a whole complicated taxonomy that I've totally forgotten now. But anyway, everybody who writes about my crimes wants to start out talking about the gymnast mutilations, because they were kinky and glamorous. So after you talk about the mutilations, do you jump back to talk about the human hay bales, or do you just drop in that information here and there? It's like the difference between a crime spree and a crime smattering. Just bear in mind how many people died to create a satisfying narrative arc, okay? Okay.

Synecdoche vs. Metonymy

Okay, so you're collecting body parts from your victims. The question is, why are you collecting them? Say you had a piano teacher who terrorized you as a child. Maybe she locked you inside the piano for hours, until you were deaf in one ear from the horrible clanging of the little felt-covered hammers. So you decide to kill women piano teachers, and to keep a little lacquer box full of their index fingers. Is that synecdoche, because the index finger stands for the whole piano teacher? Or is it metonymy, because you're keeping the fingers of women who remind you of your old teacher? I dunno. Okay, look at it this way. If you're gathering body parts because of their external symbolism—like the famous Memphis Ear-Snatcher, who only killed people whose left ears reminded him of the snails he loved with a doomed passion—then that's definitely metonymy. But if you take a piece of every fashion designer, because *Project Runway* traumatized you, then that's synecdoche. I think. The main thing is, don't collect body parts for no good reason, because that's just dumb. I have to confess something. During my mutilation phase, I had to have a toe from everyone I killed. Why? I don't know. I figured I would know what to do with them when I had enough of them. It's actually kind of embarrassing, but one day I just sat down with this pile of toes and suddenly felt like the world's biggest asshole. I mean, what are you going to do with a dozen toes? Make a toe menorah or something? I don't know. They weren't even the same kind of toe, or one of each. I was keeping them frozen, so they had a dusting of freezer burn on them, and they looked sort of like off-season strawberries. I realized there was no great art project waiting to come out of these toes. It was just the wrong medium or something. I ended up having to go out to the backyard and bury them all, and then of course my dog dug them all up a week later. I felt like such a dork reburying all those toes.

Stream of Consciousness vs. Unreliable Narrator

The star witness at my second trial had no credibility whatsoever. For one thing, he was addicted to speedballs—which, admittedly, I'd gotten him hooked on during the three months I kept him chained in my basement. And there was the sensory deprivation, interspersed with whispering snatches of Flaubert in his ear, or the faked sounds of a tea party or a rescue. The truth is, you can turn almost anyone into an unreliable narrator. It just takes a certain persistence. It's much, much harder to make someone stream of consciousness. I think most people think progressively, rather than in a stream. I know that when I'm thinking something, part of me is already thinking of the next thing I'm going to think, and maybe what I'm going to think after that. I did experiment with tape-recording one or two of my victims. I put a microphone near them and got them to say whatever came into their head. The results were really disappointing, and I have to say it's not true that pain breaks down inhibitions, or makes it any easier for people to free-associate. Even with some encouragement on my part, all I had on tape was an hour of "Please stop, it hurts." What kind of monologue is that? Talk about stating the obvious. I would have thought you'd want your last words to be something challenging or thought-provoking. But no.

Anticlimax vs. Denouement

Think of your story as a congealing pile of nun meat. Things don't always have tidy endings, unless there's a really large incinerator nearby. Just accept that things will drag on and on after you thought they should be over. I think it was John Cougar Mellencamp who had that lyric about how life goes on long after the feeling has left your extremities. The best you can hope for is some kind of narrative explosion before things peter out. Put down some tarps first, is all I'm saying.

FOREWORD FOR THE
YET-UNWRITTEN BOOK
LEAH IS A DELICATE F#%ING FLOWER*
BY AN EMOTIONALLY UNSTABLE
PERSON WITH RAGE ISSUES

by Susan Morton

That's an odd title for a book, right? But I'm a little proud of it, even though it's not my book, because, you see, it's my title. While venting to friends about some relationship problems I've been having (best not to delve into those—after all, the book isn't titled *Susan Is Codependent, Desperate for Love, and Dangerously Close to Becoming an Alcoholic*), I shouted "MOTHERF*#%ER!" at the top of my lungs in an attempt to exorcise my anger. My waifish friend Leah, easily offended by profanity, was disturbed by my Oedipal curse. Still upset from my lunchtime encounter, which included tears, shouting, and the hurried walk past of an attractive man I'd been aiming to place my newly single hopes on (which I suppose isn't going to happen now because he thinks I'm crazy at the outset rather than finding it out gradually over months of late-night phone calls, obsessive questioning, and drunken apologies—he'd have stuck around because the sex would've been awesome, in case you're wondering), I barked, "I'm sorry, I forgot: Leah is a delicate f*#%ing flower!"

Now, I'm sure many people would call me a prick and/or simply leave when that sort of comment was screamed at them without provocation. But my friends are used to my tirades and normally forgive them or tune them out. Or maybe they have some sort of masochistic psychosis that makes them seek out asswipes like me. At any rate, Leah merely laughed and said, "That should be the title of my book." Great, and I'll write the foreword. Um, what book are we talking about exactly?

Being asked to write a foreword for a book that hasn't been written is a tad tricky. What's the book going to be about? Is it fiction? Nonfiction? A gardening book with beautiful yet dull pictures? A sci-fi, fantasy-type deal about a girl who is transformed into a flower that wilts under the weight of the rain? It would be nice to know. Then I might have a clue as to the direction this foreword should take. But no, I know nothing about this book except that it hasn't been written. And it's not like I can ask the supposed author. No. She's too sensitive. She's too much of an artiste. She's too busy to answer questions about her own book. She doesn't like it when her friends vent their frustration from needy, guilt-infused lunches by cursing the emotionally retarded, passive-aggressive f*#% wit and his clingy mother. MOTHERF*#%ER! Screw this foreword! At least the title of the book is right (like it'll ever get written)—Leah is a delicate f*#%ing flower!

WHAT CRITICS AND WRITERS ARE SAYING ABOUT MY NEW BOOK OF POETRY, *THE DOBERMAN PLOT*

by Sebastian Bitticks

"Spectacular in the sense of existing somehow. Thought-filled, word-filled, sentence-filled verse."

"*The Doberman Plot* strikes a match on your eyelid and, before using it to set the cuffs of your pants on fire, asks you to consider the color of the flame."

"Sebastian Bitticks goes on record as not being a child pornographer, and, in doing so, goes on record for all of us, who are also not child pornographers."

"Slick, rain-proof stuff. Poems to paper your house with, poems that could survive a shipwreck *and* a plane crash."

"[Bitticks] stands alone among poets of our age in his enacting of interventions into the capitulations we each one posit as our response to something or other."

"*The Doberman Plot* belongs at the vanguard of the new aesthetic. You know, the shitty one."

DON'T READ THIS OR YOU MIGHT GET POKED IN THE EYE WITH A DAGGER

by Darby Larson

I wrote a novel with daggers that jut from the page and poke people in the eyes at appropriate moments in the plot. It was kind of a pop-up book, except with daggers.

The novel was about a man who was aware that all he was was a character in a novel. He hated his readers because he couldn't get away from them. He had no privacy. He was like someone on a reality television show without having signed a contract to be on a reality television show. Occasionally, he would look up and shake his fist and curse at the people reading his life. And sometimes he would poke them in the eyes with daggers.

The title of the novel was *Don't Read This or You Might Get Poked in the Eye with a Dagger.*

I used to hand out free copies to people at independently funded literary festivals. Aspiring authors smiled and said things like "Oh, you wrote this?" and "I look forward to reading it." I told them, "Please don't."

My mom found out about my novel and wanted a copy. Before shipping it, I signed the inside cover: *Mom, for the love of God, please don't read this. Love, Darby.*

After my book tour ended, my agent called and told me *Don't Read This . . .* was a breakout. It was selling like crazy. Bookstores couldn't keep them on the shelves. I said, "That's great." "Are you working on anything else?" he asked. I told him I was recording an audio version called *Don't Listen to This or You Might Get Needles Jabbed in Your Eardrums.*

My fame was overwhelming me. I had to get an unlisted number. I had to remove my e-mail address from my website. I had to buy a secluded house in the woods with a long, crazy driveway and an electronic gate at the bottom.

The university invited me to give a lecture on writing. As I walked up the cement steps to the lecture hall, a man was sitting on the steps with sunglasses on. An upturned hat lay on the ground next to him. I stopped to talk to him. He said he was blind. I asked him how he became blind. He said he was born that way.

Inside the lecture hall, I stood at a podium and told professors and aspiring writers what I thought about the craft of writing. I told them that you have to hate the readers who read your stories. You have to punish your readers. Readers want to feel pain. Then everyone murmured among themselves, "That's so true," and "You should really read his book," and they nodded in agreement and they hugged each other and they felt the happiness that agreements always bring, and then they all looked up at me with perfect eyeballs.

TEN BRIEF CHARACTER SKETCHES

by Jim Flood

1. Randy.

Can't hide his displeasure at hearing lite-instrumental renditions of songs he likes. Just the other day, he was sharing an elevator with four other people, all strangers to him, when his ears were assaulted by the Muzak version of his third-favorite song of all time, Steppenwolf's "Magic Carpet Ride." He shook his head, groaned, then closed his eyes and said out loud, "What a crappy, crappy world we live in."

2. Leanne.

Keeps her fingernails trimmed short, except the one on the middle finger of her left hand. She lets that one grow extremely long and sharp and paints garish colors and wacky patterns on it. Most of the time she thinks of it as her "fun fingernail." When she gets mad enough to flip someone off, though, it becomes her "fuck-you fingernail." Leanne often tells the story of how her "fighting fingernail" gave her the edge in her one and only no-holds-barred physical altercation. She was at the movies. A woman behind her was talking loudly. Leanne turned around to ask her to shut up, and the woman kicked the back of her seat. Out came the fighting fingernail.

3. Jonathan.

Spends as much time nude as he can. He's limited in this pursuit by the dress code at his nine-to-five office job, where he's required to wear long pants and a long-sleeve shirt, even on Fridays. Add to that a forty-five-minute clothed commute on either end of each workday and a roommate who said, "Put some fucking clothes on" the first time he walked in on Jonathan sitting nude on the couch, watching TV, and then, the second time, "If I see your naked body again, I'm kicking you the fuck out of the apartment." Jonathan has a recurring dream in which he wakes up one morning nude, as per usual, but then after showering he remains nude and goes to work that way. All the other people he encounters in the dream—pedestrians on the street, commuters on the subway, his coworkers, the waiters and other patrons at the restaurant where he eats lunch—are inspired by his nudity to take off their own clothes. Dream Jonathan navigates his way home amid the nude multitudes to find his roommate sitting on the couch, stubbornly clothed, saying, "That's it—pack up your stuff and get the hell out of here."

4. Georgia.

Makes a killer Baked Alaska, gets teary-eyed when she hears the song "California Dreamin'" and has seen the movie *Raising Arizona* twelve times. She once did an oral report on the Louisiana Purchase as a schoolchild and is currently the only nine-toed anthropologist residing in Ohio. Georgia got angry at her boyfriend Dan when he decided that road-tripping to the Kentucky Derby with a bunch of his friends was more important than accompanying her to Rhode Island for her uncle's funeral, but she forgave him the following week when he bought her a boxed set of the best episodes of *Hawaii Five-0* on VHS.

5. Bradford.

Becomes agitated if he senses that new acquaintances don't realize how smart he is; feels particularly uncomfortable around people who don't seem appropriately impressed that he went to Harvard. He generally assumes that everyone he meets is of inferior intelligence, unless he happens to know that they also graduated from an Ivy League university, but even then he almost always gives himself the benefit of the doubt, especially if they attended Cornell or Brown, which he considers the Ivies' bastard stepchildren. He typically mentions his SAT score (1520) in casual conversation three or four times a week. Anytime a person tells him something he already knows as though they think it's new to him, he becomes so unnerved that he blurts out "I know that," or "I already knew that," then bites his lip as he fights the impulse to strike the person in the face.

6. D'Ursula.

Doesn't understand why so many people her age are into the Harry Potter books. Fully mature adults, presumably capable of comprehending and enjoying works by authors who write for adults, reading children's books. It just doesn't make sense to her. She would be embarrassed if anyone saw her reading a kids' book in public, or in private for that matter. She recently quit her book discussion group, the one she cofounded, after the other members voted unanimously in favor of reading *Harry Potter and the Sorcerer's Stone*, thereby rejecting her suggestion, *The Human Stain* by Philip Roth.

7. China.

Obsessively perturbed by the idea that virtually all of the people who read her online celebrity-gossip column must think her name is pronounced like the country. It's actually pronounced Shee-na. She wishes she could include a small item in her column cluing her readers in to the correct pronunciation, but she's pretty sure her editor would strike it, because whatever limited degree of celebrity she's attained so far is not significant enough to make her worthy of a mention in her own column.

8. Ned.

Looks down almost all the time. He could talk for hours on end about floor coverings, the grooves in escalator steps, and various types of footwear, if anyone cared to listen. When walking along the streets of the city where he lives, he studies all the black blobs of filth-covered gum stuck to the sidewalks, trying, mostly in vain, to find interesting ones whose shapes remind him of farm animals or household appliances or the maps of countries he's memorized from the world atlas he keeps under his bed. He often bumps into other people, but he rarely trips and never stumbles.

9. Jeremy.

Ever jovial, his friends in Jacksonville, where he's lived all his life, know him to be an accomplished practical jokester. His former girlfriend Janine finally jilted him last July after unjustly jerking him around for years. If the Jaguars, his hometown NFL team, ever come back from a huge fourth-quarter deficit to tie the New York Jets (or, as Jeremy likes to call them, the New Jersey Jagoffs) and then beat them in overtime, he will probably jump for joy, pump his fist in the air, and yell loudly. His personal-best javelin throw in high school was just shy of a county record, a feat that earned him recognition in the yearbook as one of the "Jocks of the Year."

10. Suzette.

Hates many things: the barking of her next-door neighbor's dog, pine-scented candles, fantasy-oriented video games and the people who play them, guys named Guy, instant mashed potatoes, TV commercials for embarrassing products like yeast-infection remedies and jock-itch cream, the color yellow, Alex Trebek's mustache, kids on crutches who get in her way when she's in a hurry, free-verse poetry, Alex Trebek, the expression "it's all good" and the people who use it, the German language, and all types of lunch meats. She didn't hate the ficus tree her parents gave her for an apartment-warming gift, but she never took the time to care for it properly, and now it's dead.

AUTHOR'S LETTER TO
HIS SOON-TO-BE EX-WIFE

by Luciana Lopez

Baby, come home, please. I'm sorry—I wasn't even thinking when I gave that character your name. I guess I just love you so much that your name is always on my mind. I didn't realize that calling a cheating, drug-addicted truck-stop prostitute Torri might hurt your feelings.

After all, just because you guys have the same name doesn't mean you're the same person. Sure, you're both medium-height brunettes with blonde highlights, hazel eyes, and briefcase-shaped birthmarks on your left breasts, but that's just a coincidence. I also wrote that she was chunky around the middle, with gravity and age dragging her breasts to her knees. See? I would never say that about you.

Come back from your mother's, honey, please. You can't be happy there, the way she constantly nags at you in that whiny voice of hers. And she's probably tired of hearing you talk about all this, anyway. I'm sure she doesn't want to hear you go on and on the way you do.

Speaking of your mother, no, of course the hooker's mom isn't based on her! The names are completely different: Valeria has an *l*, Victoria has a *t*—and Torri's mom doesn't knit, she crochets. That is, streetwalker Torri, not you Torri.

And I have to object to your saying the main character is just a thinly disguised version of me. Yes, I know Bryan and Ryan are similar, but really, all my characters are totally fictional. I mean, Bryan winds up winning the lottery, divorcing Torri after he finds out what a whore she is, and becoming an international playboy. All I have in common with him is our stamp collections. Leagues apart.

Plus, Bryan's thumb-wrestling fetish is all made up. Completely.

Oh, and that bookmark? On my computer? "How to lower sperm count"? That was just research. For Bryan. My recent interest in long-distance bicycling is coincidental.

Honey, Torri, come home. What would I do without you?

P.S.: Also, I would never spike your mint lattes with mouthwash. Now you're just imagining things.

QUERY

by Tom Lombardi

I.

Dear_____ & _____ Literary Agency,

Enclosed in this very large envelope are the first two chapters of my novel, *The Whispering Monkey*, and me. *TWM* is a chilling account narrated by a precocious monkey, who, residing in a cage at the Bronx Zoo, decides to counsel his caretaker, a zookeeping divorcée, who finds herself hanging on every one of his astute words, at which point suspense, romance, and murder, not to mention aggressive page turning, ensue. In a voice at once playful and somber, *TWM* is a tale that is both haunting and full of hope.

As for me: you'll see I'm wearing a white Fruit of the Loom T-shirt ensconced in a gray sports jacket on which white pinstripes have been stitched ever so gracefully by workers in Thailand whose garment factory, according to the label, manufactures for H&M.

Lastly, due to certain postal restrictions, going barefoot was necessary. Thanks in advance for taking a look at the both of us.

Cheers,

TL

II.

Dear_____ & _____ Literary Agency,

For what seems like a considerable amount of days, my ms. and I seem to be lying under a pile of papers in what I can only assume is the storage room. Why the assumption? It's dark, and yesterday I was roused awake upon hearing someone say, "Just throw it in the storage room," at which point the door opened—fluorescent bulbs flickering above—and I yelled, "Hey!" from the confines of the large manila envelope into which my query and the first two riveting chapters of *The Whispering Monkey* and myself are stuffed; my attempt was futile, I'm afraid, for the door shut, leaving me once again in the dark and to only assume that the intern (?) responsible for tossing miscellaneous items into the storage room in haste, and thereby ignoring my plea for help, is attached to an iPod (or a similar MP3-playing device), as seems to be standard protocol among kids today.

Please note: out of respect for the fine staff at the____ & _____ Literary Agency, I fear any emerging from the storage during office hours might startle employees, as any exiting during off hours would undoubtedly trigger a security alarm. Nevertheless, a response would be much appreciated.

Regards,

TL

III.

Dear_____ & _____ Literary Agency,

It's been days since I sent you a query letter and the first two riveting chapters of my novel, *The Whispering Monkey*, and myself (as well as a follow-up letter), and yet, no response. How many days I am not sure, since I'm starting to have "spells" where I spend hours in a kind of lucid dream that involves *T.J. Hooker*—era Heather Locklear.

Apparently, no one has bothered for quite some time to open the storage room, wherein I remain in a large manila envelope. I'm tempted to flee, but I worry that the sight of a ragged stranger emerging from the storage room would only terrify an otherwise rational staff at the highly esteemed_____ & _____ Literary Agency.

I beg of you, please send someone to fish out me and my ms., *TWM* (which, I'm ashamed to admit, is slightly soiled—you can do the math), or, if nothing else, just toss in a bottle of water and perhaps a plate of what smelled like pad thai someone had microwaved or ordered yesterday.

Anxiously awaiting your response,

TL

IV.

Dear_____ & _____ Literary Agency,

Last night, I heard faint coughing emanating from other side of storage room. Have been debating since then whether to inquire aloud as to the identity of my newfound neighbor. Should a physical struggle break out, however, I fear I may lose advantage, as I appear to have lost all motor sensation in my legs. No matter. Stuffed into a large manila envelope, along with the first two engaging chapters of my novel, *The Whispering Monkey*, I await with an anticipation, I imagine, to which only a warrior could relate.

Still, can't help but wonder who *he* is, the cougher. Or is it a she? One of those leggy blondes coupled with lascivious sample chapters of chick-lit fluff? Is that what your agency is after? Reduced to targeting the *Sex and the City* demographic in search of a quick buck? More coughing. Yes, it is a woman! "Who's there?" I'm tempted to say, "Reveal yourself, you hack!" Must remain . . . integral . . .

Would appreciate a look. And maybe some of Linda's birthday cake (couldn't help but overhear the song yesterday). Please send her my birthday wishes.

Clutching the first two riveting chapters of *TWM*, waiting, waiting . . . more coughing. Oh, Jesus!

TL

V.

. . . aching belly . . . vision going. Coughing hack removed yesterday. I and query and ms. placed into container, wheeled through office. "*The Whispering Monkey* is an engaging tale woven just right for the current marketplace!" I would have said, had I not been too weary. In the elevator, lowered into parking garage. Going to an agent's apartment, I hoped. That beeping noise made when industrial truck slowly backs up. Long ride. Then: stench of sulfur. Chest stinging on each breath. Can't wiggle toes. Sound of seagulls squawking. Slow, methodical movement . . . if weren't riddled with delirium, would think I and query and sample chapters were moving along body of water. As if to confirm my suspicion, a foghorn. Oh, God! *TWM* is a riveting tale, I assure you. Thanks in advance for the look. Looking forward . . . to . . . hearing . . . from . . . you.

WORDS AND EXPRESSIONS COMMONLY MISUSED BY INSIPID BROTHERS-IN-LAW

by Dennis DiClaudio

It really IRRITATES me when people do not use proper grammar. It does not AGGRAVATE me. Do you understand that? IRRITATE means "to annoy," and AGGRAVATE means "to add to." So, if you're already IRRITATING me with your abominable speech and your insistence on smoking a cigar in my living room, your saying, "Hey buddy boy, don't get so AGGRAVATED; I'll open a window," will only AGGRAVATE the situation.

You can no more ALLUDE a former business associate whose job you procured than you can create the ALLUSION of an unprofitable year for the IRS. The words are "ELUDE" and "ILLUSION," respectively. Don't make me repeat this. You can ALLUDE to or make an ALLUSION to *The Art of War* in an e-mail, and this is quite a different thing from REFERRING to or making a REFERENCE to a specific passage from the same book, because an ALLUSION is an indirect mention, and if you just pull the whole thing off your Quote-A-Day desk calendar, it's a REFERENCE. Sometimes SpellCheck doesn't cut it. Use a dictionary.

I'm going to try to put this as simply as possible, because I realize that some people thought of English as an elective in college. "FARTHER" is a word that refers to distance. "FURTHER" refers to time or quantity. "FARTHER" has the fucking root "FAR" in it. Like "FAR away from my sister." Do not confuse these two. Note these two sentences: "My brother-in-law has his head FARTHER up his ass than I thought was humanly possible," and, "I have no FURTHER interest in hearing your opinions concerning what we should do about the city's 'Jew problem.'"

I was wondering AS TO WHETHER you are intending to offend me with your idiotic opinions or if you actually think I'll sit here and listen to this shit. AS TO WHETHER? AS TO WHETHER? What the hell is "AS TO WHETHER"? Why are you sticking an "AS TO" on the front of "WHETHER"? Just as it is unnecessary for a person to qualify every single statement with, "I'm just saying, I went to Wharton business school, and...," the "AS TO" is not needed. You're not being paid by the word. Just say "WHETHER." "WHETHER" is fine.

Think about this. Am I IMPLYING that you are a fascist, elitist prick, or can we simply INFER that from the data at hand?

In the name of everything that is good and holy, please, do not ever, ever, ever say "IRREGARDLESS" anywhere near me. What you mean to say is "REGARDLESS." REGARDLESS of whether or not you think of the English language as solely a means of ordering more sushi or bragging about your BMW, its rules must be respected, and there is no such fucking word as "IRREGARDLESS." It makes you sound even more stupid than you actually are. The prefix "IR-" is a negative. The suffix "-LESS" is a negative. How many fucking negatives do you need in one goddamned word? So help me God, I will beat the shit out of you with a tire iron.

I can't even deal with "LAY" and "LIE" right now. I'll smash something. I know it.

Do you actually mean to say that he LITERALLY dropped dead when you told him you were assuming his position in the company? Do you have any idea what you're saying? You're saying that your former boss was lying (not LAYING! not LAYING!) on the floor of his old office, with no pulse, until paramedics came and brought his lifeless body to the morgue? No, I didn't think that's what you meant. Why don't you get that dictionary and look up the LITERAL meaning of the word "LITERALLY," jerkoff?

You do realize that "THAN" and "THEN" are two different words, don't you? Do you know how you can tell? Because they're spelled differently. That "a" and "e" aren't interchangeable, you callous shitwheel. You can't just spell it how you like depending upon your mood. "I'm a stupid, fucking, big-shot stockbroker who doesn't give a shit about anybody but himself and spews his moronic opinions like vomit and probably cheats on his wife, and I think I'll spell 'THAN' with an 'e' today." No. That's not how it works, asshole! "THAN" expresses comparison and "THEN" expresses a passage of time or distance! Think of it this way: I'm literally going to grab your dick and pull it farther from your body THAN you can possibly imagine, regardless of how shrilly your screams fall upon my unsympathetic ears, until your dick comes off in my hand and I shove it down your goddamned pontificating, no-good throat! THEN we'll see whether or not you start giving the simple fucking rules of English the respect they fucking deserve!

ROUNDER CHARACTERS
IN NO TIME FLAT!

by John Warner

When I conduct my "Write Better, Write Now!" seminars all across the country, the first thing I do is ask my audience, "What is the one thing every novel needs?" The eager and uninitiated throw out answers like: "a catchy opening," "an engaging plot," or "robots," which are all true enough, but alas, are incorrect.

No, the right answer is "a compelling central character." This is true if that central character is a slightly overweight, outwardly insecure but inwardly steely singleton looking for love (*Bridget Jones's Diary*), or high-tech, extremely deadly, modern weaponry (anything by Tom Clancy).

With that in mind, here are my top five tips for creating more compelling characters.

Tip No. 1: Make your characters round, not flat.

It's important that we recognize the complexity of the human psyche when we construct our characters. Rare is the person who is all good, or all bad for that matter. The truth is, we are a mix of many different, and oftentimes contradictory traits that are in constant conflict with one another.

Consider the following two passages, and how seemingly slight changes can add nuance and mystery to a character.

> "Sister Jane walked down the alleyway. Her habit scraped the filthy ground as she grasped hands with the tiny street urchins, giving them her blessing. At the end of the block, she knelt down, bowed her head, and prayed to God to deliver sustenance to these poor souls."

vs.

> "Sister Jane walked down the alleyway. Her habit scraped the filthy ground as she grasped hands with the tiny street urchins, giving them her blessing. At the end of the block, she looked both ways before driving a boot into the ribs of a passing stray puppy."

Now, honestly, which of these passages makes you want to read on?

Tip No. 2: Give your characters some kind of superpower.

Sure, we remember Holden Caulfield as the classic, coming-of-age antihero of *The Catcher in the Rye*, but would we be as drawn to him if Salinger had neglected to give Holden the ability to kill with his thoughts?

Similarly, without the power of flight, *Lolita*'s Humbert Humbert would be just a pervert with a crush on a fourteen-year-old.

Tip No. 3: Give your characters an interesting or unusual physical characteristic.

Is it a coincidence that we remember characters such as Captain Hook, Quasimodo, or Richard Nixon so well and so fondly? No, it is not. Let me ask you this: Do you remember Frankenstein as a tragic, romantic figure, struggling to be understood amid a cruel and heartless world, or as that big green fellow with bolts in his neck?

Warning! Be wary of taking things too far, lest your characters become cartoonish and your readers begin to laugh at you. For instance, if you are writing a fantasy/sci-fi novel about a race of heroic unicorns who return to Earth in the year 3050 to liberate humanity from the great kitten enslavement, it would be wise to give Ringring, the leader of the unicorns, a jewel-encrusted horn, because who could ever forget a heroic unicorn whose horn "shines like it has rubies, or something rubylike and shiny, in it"?

However, if the unicorn also shoots laser beams from its eyes or breathes fire, you have clearly overstepped.

Tip No. 4: Make your character Hitler.
Or better yet, the cloned offspring of Hitler.

This tip is self-explanatory.

Tip No. 5: The clothes make the man (or woman).
We've just established the importance of describing physical characteristics, but it would be unwise to ignore the opportunity for characterization provided by one's mode of dress. In real life, think how often we evaluate people by what they're wearing.

Wearing white after Labor Day? Then you are hopelessly gauche. Seen sporting a fur coat? You are a murderer with no regard for animal life. Betraying a penchant for short-sleeve dress shirts? Clearly, you are Andy Sipowicz.

This technique can be especially useful for introducing minor players in the present drama, which are notoriously hard to flesh out quickly. Notice in these following examples how two wildly different supporting characters are quickly introduced through the use of novelty T-shirts.

Example 1: "As I moved toward Lex, I could see writing on his T-shirt. Bending closer, I made out the words, 'If you can read this, you must be stepping on my johnson.'"

Example 2: "As I moved toward Lex, I could see writing on his T-shirt. Bending closer, I made out the words, 'If you can read this, you are either invading my personal space, or are European.'"

Lex number one is likely to shake hands using a joy buzzer and make lewd comments about your wife, while Lex number two appears to be an individual who is sensitive to the beliefs and customs of others.

Of course, both are hopeless cretins; they are, after all, wearing novelty T-shirts.

Follow each of these tips, and you'll be on the road to success in no time. Good luck and good writing!

SUBMISSION GUIDELINES FOR OUR REFRIGERATOR DOOR

by Christopher Monks

Our refrigerator door is currently accepting your artwork, personal essays, short fiction, and poetry for submission. Please know that we are careful about the work we publish on our refrigerator door. We want people to come away from our refrigerator door feeling invigorated and alive, as if they had just learned something about themselves and/or the world that heretofore they had not.

In short, we want to provide a cathartic, life-altering experience for anybody who comes into contact with our refrigerator door. Because of this, we expect the best and only the best from those artists who wish to contribute their work.

Guidelines for Artwork

Your artwork should be strong and bold. While we are partial to realism, abstract work is okay, too, provided it is not simply abstract for the sake of being abstract. For example, you can say that squiggle in the corner of the page is a bunny, but we won't believe it is a bunny unless the artistic strength of the piece compels us to believe it is a bunny. Having floppy ears and a bushy tail always helps, too.

We are open to all types of media as long as the work is light enough to be affixed to our refrigerator door by no more than six alphabet magnets. Collages are welcome, but if the piece of art contains uncooked pasta make sure it is glued securely. Should an uncooked fusilli or farfalle detach and fall to the kitchen floor, our dog will attempt to eat it. The last time Rusty tried to eat uncooked fusilli, he nearly choked to death. That wasn't a lot of fun.

Please be sure that the work of art submitted includes the correct spelling of your first name, the date the piece was created, and a one- or two-line description of the piece. We realize some artists don't like to include descriptions of their work because they find it "boring and dumb" to have to write them, but we find descriptions essential because sometimes we have no idea what it is we're looking at.

Guidelines for Personal Essays and Fiction

Your writing must explode off the page and render the reader your helpless, quivering slave. As stated earlier, our refrigerator door is in the life-changing business, so be sure to pack your prose with power, grace, and proper use of punctuation. Commas are not little playthings that you can leave here, there, and everywhere. So use them wisely or don't use them at all. Same goes for exclamation points.

We prefer all written work to be submitted on either white-lined or yellow-lined paper. The color of paper doesn't really matter, but it's imperative you use lined paper with proper margins. Far too often we receive submissions that are nothing more than long scribbles written haphazardly over the entire page. In the past we've found this style to be sweet and charming in its simplicity, but we now require work that is aesthetically more grown-up-looking.

Submissions should be no more than a page long. There is only so much space to go around our refrigerator door, as there must be room for the grocery shopping list, random family photos, and that invitation to the wedding we are dreading having to attend. Double-sided work will not be considered. We don't want readers lifting work to view content on the other side of the paper. Everything is precarious enough as it is, what with the weak-holding alphabet magnets.

Guidelines for Poetry

We are open to poetry, but keep in mind that any poem containing the word "poop" or variations of the word, such as "poopy," "poopsicle," or "pooptastic," will not be considered for publication. No one wants to read about poop while standing at our refrigerator door. We recommend you submit your poopy poem to the bathroom wall instead.

Special Note Regarding Robot Monkeys

We are no longer accepting Robot Monkey–themed work, be it drawings, stories, or whatever. We've had it up to here with Robot Monkeys. Yes, Robot Monkeys are "funny" and "cool" and they make "amazing" beeping sounds, but enough is enough with the Robot Monkeys. Robot Monkeys are so last July. And no saying that something is a tree and then later telling us it's a Robot Monkey. That will lead to immediate removal from our refrigerator door, and no amount of crying and spinning wildly on the floor will make us put it back up.

No Simultaneous Submissions

We understand that you have many choices for publication. Nannie and Pop-Pop's refrigerator door, your teacher's bulletin board, your babysitter's high-school locker, and Uncle Todd's full-length mirror are all fine places to display your work. However, we ask that you refrain from submitting to more than one place at a time. We don't wish to relive the turmoil we had with Nannie and Pop-Pop over your "Fat Elephant Skateboarding at the Beach" piece.

Three Questions You Must Ask Yourself
Before Submitting Your Work

Have I spelled my name correctly on my submission?

Is my submission Robot Monkey–free?

Does my submission seek to make a difference in people's lives?

We thank you for considering our refrigerator door for publication of your work. Please allow a one-to-three-minute response time for your submission. If we are busy watching *Prison Break*, expect a slightly longer wait time. Go clean the playroom or something. Just leave us alone and let us watch our show until it's over.

WHY I WON'T SELL YOUR MEMOIR TO HOLLYWOOD FOR MILLIONS, GRANDMA

by Amelia Morris

Mostly because I'm in no position to do so. I'm a receptionist at a music school.

Partly because I know you gave this memoir to all the men in our extended family before you gave it to me, since you consciously, though not vocally, think that women are incapable man-garnishes. I know the only reason I am now getting this memoir is because I now live in Hollywood and you think I must know some big-time producers.

Partly because it's not even a script. It's a handwritten journal that you Xeroxed.

Partly because no one in the family believes you were kidnapped and taken to Mexico by your ex-boyfriend. The others who read the memoir told me what really happened—you went with him willingly on a vacation, but then wanted to get back together with Grandpa, so you called Grandpa from Mexico and told him you'd been kidnapped.

Partly because you keep calling me at horrible times (5 a.m., 6 a.m.)

and leaving horribly droning messages about how we are both going to be millionaires because of your memoir, which your girlfriends all agree is better than anything that's in the theaters, and how you sent it via UPS and how I should keep my eyes open for it because you only have so many copies of it. When I did call you back to tell you I had received the memoir and to please not call at those times, you blamed the time difference, but the time difference is quite nice, especially when I wake up on Sunday and my favorite football team is kicking off at 10 a.m. So I couldn't possibly place the blame there.

Partly because when I told you that I didn't think I'd be able to do anything with the memoir, you said, "I'll bet you didn't even read it," and hung up on me.

Partly because you've been a bit of an asshole-grandma. This is the first time you've called me regularly in my entire life. I guess it's all relative, but I prefer my other grandma, who is as sweet as they come. Just the other day I called her and she was making cinnamon buns for the neighbors who had just brought their new baby home from the hospital. Now that's a grandma.

Partly because—oh, Grandma, fuck it. I'm in. I'll make some phone calls and we'll publish your memoir and celebrate the forthcoming millions by eating foie gras doused in pints of truffle oil.

TWIST ENDINGS

by Geoff Haggerty

It was a dream.
He was a girl.
She was a guy.
He did it.
He wasn't real.
He was dead the whole time.
She was dead the whole time.
They were dead the whole time.
It was aliens.
It was robots.
It was science fiction.
God did it.

JEAN-PAUL SARTRE,
911 OPERATOR

by Tyler Smith

OPERATOR

911. What is your *urgence?*

CALLER

Operator, I need an ambulance. I think I just cut my finger off in the blender...

OPERATOR

(The sound of a cigarette being lit, then an exhale.)

CALLER

Do you hear me, man! I need an ambulance at 2304 Powell Street now!

OPERATOR

Ceci s'intéresse. Yes, the predicament of Roquentin...yes...it is the indifference to existence of the inanimate. No matter how much he longs for something other or something different, he cannot get away from the plundering evidence of his engagement with the world. You know, *le Monde*. I think we must look at...

CALLER

What in the shit are you talking about? I was just making margaritas...

OPERATOR

Ah, oui. Vous pensez. A typical ignorance of the common folk. Perhaps this is why you sit with your extremity half-digested in the bowels of the blender. It seems you are...*comment devoir je dis*...a student of Kant? Freedom. I spit.

CALLER

I think I'm going to pass out...*(Click.)*

* * *

OPERATOR

911. What is your *urgence?*

CALLER

Oh, God. Oh, no. I think my husband is dying. He's grabbing his chest. I think...I think he's having a heart attack. Operator, he's turning blue!

OPERATOR

(Chortles contemptuously.) Mort inévitable. Oui. Oui. Depriving life of meaning. You must know you cannot await his death. *Vous devez savoir,* because meaning can exist only insofar as there is a future toward which one can project oneself, death deprives such...

CALLER

It's his heart, operator. Oh, please help him. Send an ambulance. I love you, Herbert! Operator, *please*! I love him so much...

OPERATOR

Do you have a second?

CALLER

Wha...?

OPERATOR

Look, madame. Take a deep breath. *Êtes-vous relâché?* Good. Now, think of the heart as a rock, or a small pumpkin. A heart cannot be anything else than a heart, but if a man comes along, that man can use it as a weapon. And now, you see, the heart is back to its ideal state. You are safe. And what of this love? You play the part of grieving subject in a case where subjectivity is traded off between persons like a hot *pomme de terre*. Relax. Travel. Rocamadour is nice this time of year. Or La Rochelle.

CALLER

Operator, I *need* help, here. Herbert's not moving. He's everything to me... Help us...

OPERATOR

Je vous aide, madame. Trust me, this helps. Where was I? Oh, *oui*... an anticipation of the very meaning of consciousness and subjectivity. This illusory shared consciousness stands as a pointed reminder of our inability to achieve oneness with the other. So, we have a man whose heart is *mort*, black. That is all we have. How nau-se-ating. *(Chuckles.)* It is only by nature of your *décision* that this news should be important to me. *Peux-je vous demander quelque...*

CALLER

Herbert! *(Click.)*

* * *

OPERATOR

911. What is your *urgence?*

CALLER

Hello? What? Hello?

OPERATOR

Que voulez-vous? What do you *want?*

CALLER

I think there's an intruder in my house. Will you send the police? Please. Please hurry.

OPERATOR

Putain! I have said before, Man is not the sum of what he has already, but rather the sum of what he does not yet have, of what he could have. Hmm, I wonder how I feel about things he once had but now doesn't, or won't—I am referring to this intruder, *bien sûr.* Man is anguish. Doors open. Structures like poverty have the literal agency of the component, individual human being, but this class structure is a *destine* and we can speak cogently of social forces which bring to bear causality and turn us into *esclaves*—you know...slaves. This is a truism. A must for *humanité.* Or at least for *frère* breaking and entering, *non?*

CALLER

I swear to God, man. You've gotta do something. Are you speaking French or something? Are you even listening to me, man? I think this guy may be coming up the stairs. Oh, God, I'm scared. Please send *somebody.*

OPERATOR

Appropriating by destruction. Such horror. But, as they say in greeting cards, *À coeur vaillant rien d'impossible.* What a load! But I don't mean to upset you, you know that, eh?

CALLER

He's outside my fucking door! Who is this?

OPERATOR

(Long drag off a cigarette.) Jean-Paul.

CALLER

Huh?

OPERATOR

J'ai dit Jean-Paul. Look here, monsieur. Has it occurred to you that all which we abandon, all that we give, we enjoy in a higher manner through the fact that we give it away. *Pour donner* is to enjoy possessively the object which one gives. Sit back. Take a bath, *peut-être.*

CALLER

He's banging on my fucking door, man! *(Click.)*

* * *

OPERATOR

911. Vat iss your emergency?

CALLER

There's an intruder at my door. Right now he's here. I'm so scared. Look, you've got to hurry up because... You're not French, are you?

OPERATOR

Ach, mein Gott... Does "Wittgenstein" sound French to you?

ROUGH DRAFTS
OF JENNA BUSH'S
YOUNG-ADULT NOVEL

by Jeff Burnosky

Are You There, God? It's Me, Jenna

Are you there, God? It's me, Jenna. We're moving today and I'm so scared. Suppose I hate being the daughter of the leader of the free world? Suppose he does a horrible job with everything he touches and, like, the whole world hates him? Please, God, don't let Daddy's presidency be catastrophic and stuff. Thank you.

We moved to Washington today, in the middle of January. Ugh, it's so cold. I'm afraid Daddy's nipples will totally be showing when he's reciting the State of the Inauguration or whatever it is. Mommy wants me to wear a strapless dress, but then some of Daddy's friends accused me of having a sinful lust for increasing my bust. It's sort of true! I hope I don't get my period during Inaugural Ball. I tried to talk to my Daddy about it, but he said he was never that good at grammar.

The Insiders

"Are you okay, My Little Pony Girl?"

Diet Soda Pop was shaking me and I wished she'd stop, because I'd done at least twelve Jell-O shots at the Wild Stallion on Sixth Street last night and I was hungover something fierce.

I've been a soc ever since my great-grandfather first wanted to have children that were born into ridiculous wealth and unearned, or undeserved, access to power and influence.

Diet Soda got her breath and started to tell the story.

"Greasers," she said. "The greasers started a rumble. Mary's hurt bad."

I started to remember the time that Mary, Diet Soda, and I were at Camp David and she accidentally started to become a lesbian and we were all worried that meant she was actually a greaser. Then we worried about her dad, and told her that being a lesbian would totally hurt her dad in the southern and midwestern states.

"Don't do it. For Cheney," we said.

But it was too late and pretty soon the greasers were constantly chasing us, writing articles, and talking about us on *The View.* At night, as I tried to lose myself in tortured sleep, I kept hearing the last words Mary ever said to me before she went into hiding.

"Stay the course," she said. "Stay the course, Pony Girl."

Harry Potter and the Wand of Betterness

Harry was the first to awake in the White House that morning. He got up, looked around, and slipped into the Oval Office. It was 9 a.m. on a Tuesday, far too early for anyone else to wake up or for anything important to happen.

He sat down at the president's desk and spun around in the big leather chair. As he spun, he started to worry about all the terrible things that were happening in the world, especially the constant, persistent, never-ceasing risk of bad people hurting good people. He opened the desk drawer, pulled out a wand, and waved it in the air, hoping to cure all the problems. And it worked. All the problems magically went away. No terrorism, no global warming, no hideous wars with no end.

The president walked in the room and gave him a big hug.

"You figured it out, Harry," the president said with a smile. "I've been waving that wand at the desk for six years. I guess I was just doing it wrong."

"It's easy, Mr. President. I just loosened it up for you."

"Thanks, Harry!"

"It just goes to show you: the best thing to do in any situation is to persist, even in the face of futility and tragedy, for six years if you have to, and then one day someone will come along and make everything better!"

"That's what she said!"

The Fledgling Democracy of the Traveling Pants

Somehow all of the girls and I made our way to Baghdad. It was so hot! We looked at each other and laughed because we were all thinking the same thing.

"It's almost like we don't need pants!" Britt said.

"Especially since it's not a civil war," Heather said.

"And what would traveling pants do for us when things are clearly on the upswing?" Audrey said.

"Wow! What this place could really use is a whole bunch more soldiers who have traveling pants."

"But light ones, because it's hot."

Suddenly, a troop of 21,000 really hot soldiers passed in front of us. Again, we all thought the same thing.

"I'd greet them as liberators!" Julianna giggled.

"Of my traveling pants!" we all said.

We all laughed and looked toward the bright future full of vitality and security.

WHALE OF MASS DESTRUCTION— RICHARD B. CHENEY, ADJUNCT PROFESSOR IN THE HUMANITIES, PRESENTS: THE ANNUAL SYMBOLISM IN MELVILLE LECTURE

by Blair Becker

I. The Characters

A. STARBUCK: Obedient and competent first mate. Willing to do the bidding of the administration without question. Open to taking a fall. A good man to have around. Experiences some bitterness toward the end of his tour, but unflinchingly performs duty to the end.

B. STUBB: A veteran of his profession, the second mate remains unaffected during times of extreme stress. Some say he fails to grasp the gravity of desperate situations and relies too heavily on an escapist sense of humor. Though he can unleash a cruel tongue at times, history will show that he is the greatest second mate in the history of whaling.

C. FLASK: Simpleminded and passionate third mate. Though he's never thrown a harpoon, Flask enjoys commanding the charge. He's often seen running up and down the side deck in search of his beloved flying sea cucumbers. His confused rhetoric, liberal doses of noontime grog, and premature pronouncements of victory on the poop deck are liabilities, but he sticks to his convictions, and middle-Nantucket whaling folk respect that.

D. AHAB: Fearless and visionary captain. Not often seen above deck, this mastermind reengineers the way ships and whaling expeditions will be run forever. A lifelong servant to the larger whaling syndicate, Ahab takes it upon himself to make the oceans safer by ridding the world of its ultimate evildoer (with whom he had an earlier, prematurely concluded skirmish). Pursues WMD around the globe, while managing an ungrateful and mutinous crew, and without the slightest convenience or emergency medical device from home. Incredible.

E. ISHMAEL: Indecisive intellectual who is afraid to commit to the job at hand. Full of wishy-washy apprehensions and reflective moments of insight. Bi-curious episode in Nantucket with large ethnic friend all but confirmed. A true weak link. Luckily, Ishmael has been stripped of any power and is too timid to voice complaint. A true captain would hang this insurgent from the yardarm, but, as usual, this would cause Flask to lose his standing with the men. Luckily, a ship in international waters is not under standard legal constraints and Ishmael can be placed in the hold, where buckets of water are dumped on his head in an unrelenting fashion.

II. Historical Background
A. Moby-Dick, whale of mass destruction, swimming through the seas unchecked, consorting with reefs, hurricanes, and any number of cataloged hazards to navigation. WMD has rebuked international whale inspectors for years.

B. A tyrant to his own race, WMD perpetrates indiscriminate crimes upon all factions of sperm whales.

C. Held alleged meeting in 1836 with the iceberg that went on to sink the steamship *Lady of the Lake.* There were, of course, no survivors.

D. WMD now actively pursuing a rare uranium-capping treatment in Africa for his eighty teeth in order to deliver a "dirty bite" to vessels engaged in the whaling trade. (HIGHLIGHT THIS POINT in your notes.)

E. Recruited a large number of sharks to serve as mobile weapons labs to disperse large amounts of concentrated jellyfish poison. Intelligence estimates put the amount at five billion tons of jellyfish juice per shark.

F. Bottom line: this whale is really giving people the runaround.

III. Plot

A. With the support of a secretive and religious minority, the fearless Ahab rises to power (refer to above character description) and vows to rid the world of WMD, thus bringing peace and democracy to the world's oceans. Some speculate that he is hell-bent on eliminating WMD in order to procure massive amounts of whale oil. This impression is not helped by Ahab's disregard for criticism voiced by fellow whaling captains. Theory soundly debunked (KEY POINT) by Ahab's many moving speeches discussing the larger goal of liberating all whales and fish and creating a free and democratic undersea nation.

B. Ahab is at first successful in raising support for the effort by nailing a large ransom sum to the mast and distributing playing cards depicting the most grievous of spermaceti offenders. The harddriving dedication of Ahab's quest unfortunately proves too much for the crew, and their lack of support and premonitions of disaster ultimately doom the mission to failure.

C. (IMPORTANT: Guaranteed to show up on the midterm!) Had he been given supreme executive command and been able to shed the shackles of merchant maritime law, Ahab certainly would have destroyed WMD.

ROMEO AND JULIET FLYNN, THE SOPHOMORE SQUAD'S HEAD CHEERLEADER

by Jean-Pierre LaCrampe

(Verona High's evening study hall.)

ROMEO

Her eyes in heaven
Would through the airy region stream so bright
That birds would sing and think it were not night.
See how she leans her cheek upon her hand!
O, that I were a glove upon that hand,
That I might touch that cheek!

JULIET

Shut up, retard. You get near my cheek and I'll rip your airy region out.

ROMEO

She speaks.

O, speak again, bright angel, for thou art
As glorious to this night, being o'er my head,
As is a wingèd messenger of heaven...

JULIET

I said *shut up*, retard. You smell like Doritos. And do you *mind* sitting a
little farther away? I can feel your stupid Dorito breath on my face.

ROMEO

Shall I hear more, or shall I speak at this?

JULIET

Listen, creepoid, my older brother's a linebacker on the varsity squad—
and he just *loves* to beat up the creepoids that bother me.

ROMEO

I take thee at thy word!

JULIET

I know you: Hienkles, right? Your sister's a bitch. Did you know that,
Nacho Breath? You're related to a walrus-faced ho-sack.

ROMEO

My name, dear saint, is hateful to myself
Because it is an enemy to thee.
Had I it written, I would tear the word.

JULIET

Whatevs. Don't you play tuba in the stupid jazz band, or something even gayer, like the oboe?

ROMEO

Neither, fair maid, if either thee dislike.

JULIET

You're weirding me out, Cheese 'Stache. And you better not be the sicko that's been peeking into my bedroom window—my dad and brothers are going to crunch the cookies out of that guy.

ROMEO

Thy kinsmen are no stop to me.

JULIET

Okay. Let me just *explain* something: my older brother benches, like, 325—in his sleep. With the flu. Plus, my dad has a collection of crazy-sharp Japanese swords that he got from the emperor or somebody. Like fifteen of them.

ROMEO

Alack, there lies more peril in thine eye
Than twenty of their swords.

JULIET

My brothers are going to shit *honey* over this. You know it's tough playing the oboe with broken thumbs, don't you?

ROMEO

My life were better ended by their hate
Than death proroguèd, wanting of thy love.

JULIET

Jeez, could your fingernails be any longer? You disgust me. Go away.

ROMEO

Wert thou as far
As that vast shore washed with the farthest sea,
I should adventure for such merchandise.

JULIET

Shut up. And why is your hair so greasy? God, you're grosser than a bag of bear shit. Go tell Blake to come over here. And *move* to where I can't smell your corn chips and hair juice.

ROMEO

O, wilt thou leave me so unsatisfied?

JULIET

Seriously, what do you want to leave me alone?

ROMEO

Th' exchange of thy love's faithful vow for mine.

JULIET

Okay...Fine.
I...I...love you.
...*Not.*
God, you're so stupid and gross.
You dumb oboe player.

ROMEO

Wouldst thou withdraw it? For what purpose, love?

JULIET

Because your fingers are orange,
And you smell like fake cheese.
How many bags of Doritos did you eat? Like ten?
Oh, my God! Are you *crying*?
What are you crying for, you stupid baby?
Hey, Blake! Blake, listen:
Hienkles sounds just like a blubbering walrus.

Arrf, arrf, arrf.
Arrf, arrf, arrf.

Okay, that's enough—
It's not really funny anymore.
Jeez, you know, even for a stalker, you're really emotional. Now here:
shut up and do my civics homework.

ROMEO

O blessèd, blessèd night! I am afeard,
Being in night, all this is but a dream,
Too flattering-sweet to be substantial.

JULIET

I said *shut up*, retard.

(Exeunt.)

YESTERDAY'S BOOK REPORTS
FROM TODAY'S NOTABLES

by Wayne Gladstone

Alice in Wonderland, by Matt McConaughey, October 14, 1985

Alice in Wonderland is about this girl's trippy adventures in a far-out place called "Wonderland." There are all these weird dudes running around. Like there's this freaky Cheshire cat and even a caterpillar smoking a hookah. No, really. A hookah. That's in the movie. I mean, the book. I read the book.

My favorite part is where Alice sees some cake that has a sign that says "Eat me." "Eat me!" The sign says "Eat me." Seriously.

After Alice goes on a few more "trips," she meets this total buzz-kill queen who's, like, all about harshing everyone's mellow. She sucks. If I were Alice, I'd tell the queen to smoke some of that caterpillar's hookah.

Anyway, then she wakes up and everything's over. The book was pretty cool, but I don't think it's cool that this Lewis Carroll ripped off Jefferson Airplane's "White Rabbit." I mean, not cool at all, y'know? That song has a caterpillar and a queen in it, too. And it rocks.

The Jungle, by Ralph Nader, December 2, 1951

The Jungle by Upton Sinclair details corporate America's abuses in the meat-packing industry. The book, published in 1906, caused a major uproar and led to the passage of the Pure Food and Drug Act that same year. At one point in the book, a factory worker falls into a meat grinder, but the plant processes the meat anyway. Supposedly, that doesn't happen anymore, but I still think Sinclair was a failure. The Pure Food and Drug Act doesn't do nearly enough. And it seems corporate America has only gotten worse.

Sinclair also ran for Congress unsuccessfully a few times. If he really wanted to make a difference, he should have run for president. He still would have lost, but hopefully he could have frustrated the campaign of a good and qualified man, thereby saddling this stupid country with a horrible president to punish apathetic Americans for their indifference. Anyway, someone should do that.

A Separate Peace, by Matt Damon, February 8, 1986

I really related to this book. It's about two best friends who go to a respected New England school: an earnest, responsible student named Gene and a carefree, inexplicably successful student named Finny. Even though it didn't make any sense to me that a guy like Finny could go to a respected New England school, I still liked this book. Especially the part where Gene pushes Finny out of a tree and Finny breaks his leg.

Finny is too busy having fun to notice that there's evil in the world. He doesn't even believe Gene when Gene confesses to pushing Finny out of the tree on purpose. That actually works out great, because Finny runs away and breaks his leg again. But this time marrow enters his bloodstream and kills him. I think this means that people who are too lazy and irresponsible to know what's going on deserve to die, even if they're your friend. And that people who study hard and go to good schools will be successful even if they're friends with an idiot they wish were dead.

The Trial, by Chris Hansen, October 12, 1982

This book by Franz Kafka is about a man, Josef K., who is ultimately executed for some crime. We never learn what that crime is, and the book starts with the author telling us that Josef K. was arrested because someone was "spreading rumors" about him.

Still, people don't come looking for you unless you've done something wrong, right? I think Franz Kafka never tells the reader what Josef K. did because the book was published in 1925 and you probably couldn't talk about sex crimes back then. I mean, it seems pretty obvious that Josef K. was propositioning teens for sex. Why else would he be held up to ridicule in front of his landlady, family, and employer without the benefit of any kind of legal representation?

At one point in the book, Josef K. speaks out against the system that sits in judgment of him. But that's precisely how you know he's guilty. I liked this book a lot. It made me feel good because I'm not Josef K.

JANE EYRE RUNS FOR PRESIDENT

by Sean Carman

I am challenged at the Iowa caucuses to endorse gay marriage as a sacred institution. Of course I believe it, but how can they make me say so when they know the political cost it will exact? Hot tears of rage stream down my scarlet face.

In New Hampshire, I endure the grandiose posturing of Chris Matthews so I can get an interview on MSNBC. What a blowhard the man is! Who, man or woman, would not find his pompous questions exasperating? I curl my fists into tiny balls beneath the interview table.

There comes a time, dear reader, when a woman of high conscience must make her feelings plain. Today, in Ohio, I came out strongly for government support of stem-cell research.

I am for an increase in the minimum wage. I believe the government should negotiate with pharmaceutical companies to lower the cost of prescription drugs. I am curious as to why there are not more books of quality in the nation's public libraries. I have taken fewer liberties on the campaign trail than others have, surely, but this small conservatism is a wise choice for a woman of my stature in a fight to gain the highest office in the land.

Reader, take this information and hold it to your heart. It is between us. I am in love with the person who will likely be my running mate, the future vice president. He is a young senator from Illinois with a handsome countenance, the most remarkable pedigree, and an unfortunate middle name. What ever shall I do!

I am determined not to allow Senator McCain, of the state of Arizona, to escape responsibility for the abandonment of his principles. My campaign has released a list of talking points. The main theme is that McCain will say anything to get elected.

We are in the "swing" states. Curious nomenclature these Americans use. I sometimes think language is not their strong suit. Plans for the convention are coming along. My senator looks well before the crowds. Handsome, sure of himself, and quite tall. I do quite like him. We make a pair.

In other matters, a midnight rendezvous with the young senator has left me flushed. So dizzy was I, it's a wonder I made it back to my room. Today, I could barely keep my mind on my stump speech. The campaign is in constant motion. Everything is a blur. Our consultants tell us Georgia and Florida are well in hand.

In South Carolina, my nemesis McCain makes an issue of my lack of military service. He appears oblivious to the fact that nineteenth-century Englishwomen were prohibited from military service. So I ask him, "If I have no military experience, what fault is that of mine?" Does he not see the injustice of his charge, at least as it relates to me? Truly, a young woman of courage has few friends in this world.

The papers today have released a secret the senator and I have shared, and our advisers fear it imperils our campaign. The senator and I, it has been revealed, both speak French, and sometimes converse in that language. What of it? Is this all the opposition has? I have told my senator not to worry. Common sense will, in the end, prevail.

Dear reader, it has been a whirlwind! Never have I known any task to be so arduous, or so prolonged. But New York has put us over the top. To my mind, this is just according to plan. The young senator and I may now plan our convention. The event will be more a coronation than a nomination, but such is the trend, and I see no harm in following it.

There will be time enough for change, dear reader. Fret not about your little Jane.

Oh, we are to win, dear reader, we are to win! I can sense it in my heart. McCain is too old. The campaign has scarcely begun and already he is faltering. We're up by three points, and our lead can only grow. It is a new era in American politics. The permanent Republican majority is truly cooked, and I will be the first nineteenth-century Victorian woman president. Imagine!

I can already see myself, with my hand upon the Bible that will be held by Chief Justice Roberts, which is unfortunate, but what can one do? They can't be fired. Still, the image appeals, and beyond it I can see the bright future my young senator and I, and our country, will share. An increase in the minimum wage. Lower prices for prescription drugs. An end to the horrid occupation of Iraq. Finally, and thank God.

We are like a lamp atop the tall mast of a ship, the senator and I, and the American people are the wind that fills our sails. I am so fortunate to have been a good speechwriter. The senator and I are quite a team. We have been blessed with the mercy of heaven, a strong political mandate, and a majority in both houses.

He is like the country he loves so much: towering, confident, not always as articulate as you would expect. He should probably run for the office himself someday. But, until then, I shall lead them both, my love and my country, for as long as they will let me, and when they put their collective arm around me I shall be their prop and their guide.

THRILLING CHAPTER ENDINGS
YOU MAY USE IN YOUR
NEXT NOVEL

by Zhubin Parang

"Hold everything!" Dr. Hiller shouted as he burst into the room. "[PROTAGONIST'S NAME], my studies conclusively prove that you've been dead this entire time!"

As [MALE PROTAGONIST] and [FEMALE PROTAGONIST] shared their first kiss, [MALE PROTAGONIST] slowly lowered his hand from her face and gently cupped her breast, then her other breast, then, to his astonishment, yet another breast.

Suddenly, [PROTAGONIST] noticed darting shadows in the corner of the ballroom. Ninjas!

"Wait a minute," said [PROTAGONIST]. "So, as I understand it, [RECAP MAJOR PLOT POINTS OF NOVEL SO FAR]?"
"Yes," replied [MINOR CHARACTER].

"By the way," [PROTAGONIST] said with a knowing smile, "did I happen to mention that I'm black?"

[PROTAGONIST] grimly shook his head, knowing that his plan was not working, and also that the person reading this book has no idea that right now there is a *Mad About You* marathon on TV.

Note: This is a long shot, but if it works, the reader will be totally freaked out.

"Does this mean we're breaking up?" [MALE PROTAGONIST] asked, struggling to keep his voice from breaking.

"I think so," [FEMALE PROTAGONIST] whispered, as tears rolled down her cheek. "I just think we've grown apart...I'm so sorry."

[MALE PROTAGONIST] slowly nodded, and his thoughts briefly flitted to the day they first met, that summer after freshman year, when the world seemed to BOO!

Note: Ideally, this ending should be used in conjunction with some sort of timed firecracker device hidden in the book's binding. Talk to your publisher.

The crowd suddenly hushed. There, in the doorway, stood the evil Colonel Maldefore.

Note: Colonel Maldefore does not need to be a major character in your novel for this ending to work. In fact, the thrilling effect may be greater if he just randomly shows up every now and then.

[PROTAGONIST] walked down the shore. The wind was howling, and the first drops of rain had begun to splatter into the sand.

Note: On the opposite page is a notice from the government stating that the act of purchasing your novel has bound the reader to a two-year term of service in the U.S. Army. The reader is ordered to appear at the nearest recruiting office within twenty-four hours.

POSSIBLE TITLES FOR
FUTURE SUE GRAFTON NOVELS
AFTER SHE RUNS OUT OF LETTERS

by Chris Steck

"/" Is for Slash
"F1" Is for Help
"," Is Almost for Coma
"#" Is for #27
"^" Is for Caret-id Artery
"~" Is for Tilde-ath
"Ctrl+X" Is for Cut
":" Is for Colon Cancer... or Is It?

I SEE NO OTHER OPTION THAN TO RESIGN AS EMILY DICKINSON'S RAP-BATTLE COACH

by Tyler Smith

Dear MC Emmie-D,

Let me first admit that last weekend's debacle was partially my fault. My decision to sign you up for a rap battle with MC Killah Klawz was a bit premature, as we may have overestimated your familiarity with the genre. Nevertheless, I thought we had enough lyrical ammo for you to at least hold your own up there, but obviously I was wrong. With that said, I do think much of the blame falls on your shoulders. Just what prompted that sartorial train wreck of yours? I thought we agreed that you'd rock the peanut-butter Tims and the Fubu sweatsuit I had custom-fitted for you at Jimmy Jazz on West 125th. But no: you show up with your hair in a bun, rocking a Victorian brocade dress with a full front bodice, cartridge pleats, and a bunch of frills. This kind of thing may be de rigueur up in Amherst, but we don't roll like that in Brooklyn.

Then there's the issue of the battle itself. Now, MC Killah Klawz can off top flow, but he's not unbeatable. I mean, when he came at you with the whole agoraphobia angle, "This bitch ain't left the house / since 1845 . . ," I thought you might reply with something about his "jacked-up grill" or all his illegitimate babies, but instead you inexplicably spit back:

> Because I could not stop for Death—
> He kindly stopped for me [this actually sounded kind of promising
>   at first]—
> The Carriage held but just Ourselves—
> And Immortality.

Carriages? What does that mean? You didn't even try to step to him. Just you and Death riding around in some carriage. You could have at least had the carriage rolling on twenties.

Even with round one going to MC Killah Klawz, I thought you'd eventually step up like a champion. Instead, you just droned on about flies buzzing when you died, as if you were off in your own private world. Were you trippin', Emily? Didn't you remember what I said? I said to win a rap battle you needed three things: metaphors, disses, and humor. It's a pretty easy formula. All we had to do was flip the script of Killah Klawz, and we could have salvaged some dignity and walked out of there with our heads held high. Instead, you dropped:

> The Dews drew quivering and chill—
> For only Gossamer, my Gown—
> My Tippet—only Tulle.

What the hell was that? "Tippets" and "Tulles"? Are those, like, rival gangs in Amherst, or did you just panic up there? You also may be the only person ever to reference "dew" in a rap battle. Your extempore anecdotes recalling your time at Mount Holyoke weren't quite the hit you thought they were, either. Let's face it: the whole thing was a total disaster.

Emily, I like you. I really do. I think you have a fertile mind and may one day make a name for yourself on the spoken-word circuit, but the rap game clearly is not for you. I apologize for trying to rush you out there with all the hype and the lights and the pressure. (I also think we could have come up with a much better rap handle than MC Emmie-D.) Simply put, you weren't ready, and for that I apologize. I will, of course, waive my fee and wish you the best in all your future endeavors.

It was great getting to know you, and I really do hope our paths cross again sometime soon. Please take this week's break in correspondence as nothing more than a simple attempt on my part to "regroup." Some things just weren't meant to be, d'accord?

No hard feelings,
MC T-Smitty (ret.)

P.S. This past week, I've been working with a young rapper named Sylvia Plath. She's a little rough around the edges and definitely volatile, but I think she's got some real potential. Sylvia (MC Sylvie-P?) has got a battle coming up in a week, and I think you might really enjoy it. If you can talk yourself out of the house, take the bus down to NYC, ring my cell and I'll holla back.

HOLDEN CAULFIELD GIVES THE COMMENCEMENT SPEECH TO HIS HIGH SCHOOL

by Andrew Tan

You're all a bunch of goddam phonies.

GREGOR SAMSA, COACH

by Will Layman

C'mon, now. C'mon, let's take care of the ball, now. Look to post up. Look for Steve in the paint—c'mon. Yes. Now, box out! Box!

"Stands" by using front legs to climb up a metal-legged chair to a forty-five-degree angle, rising several feet in the air—a good five, six feet if you count the gesticulating antennae, sniffing wildly, which pick up the scent of a potential mate.

All right, drop back—zone trap, blue! Arms out, guys—cut off the passing lanes! Freaking BOX OUT! Come on! What's goin' on, now? Aren't you guys even listening to me? Jesus!

Throws clipboard to ground, wriggles off sport coat, and subtly extrudes a greenish film from his salivary glands.

They're gonna press the inbounds pass, fellas! C'mon, now—stack up and break! Let's go!

The ball, squirting loose, bangs into Coach Samsa's chair, knocking him to his side and then, in the slow rocking motion of an upended dome, onto his exoskeletal back.

I can't believe it! Did you guys come to play or just to mess around? Do we run these plays each day in practice, or am I dreaming? Actually, I'm in a freaking nightmare! I'm dying here. Time out! Someone get me a towel. Time out!

More rocking back and forth, then incessant guttural clicking until halftime.

BORGES WAS A WEBELO

by Benjamin Cohen

I joined the Cub Scouts to find the sound of color. Our adventures were palimpsests, the light across my yellow scarf, the yellow scarf across my starved soul, each marking over the other. Plus, there were Game Boys. We put in our time, Troop 63, earning our badges. Bobcat, check. Bear, check. Wolf, check. Mr. Wilkerson was our den leader. He was far more, this noble gatekeeper.

Soon, I crossed the bridge below the clouded arc near the flow by the waters of cavernous time. I began my path toward the Webelo. Left at Tlon, straight past the Chuck E. Cheese on Telegraph, then right at Uqbar, I imagined.

My Scout Book said this: "Collecting and identifying rocks can be great fun. It might even lead to a job in geology." Spinoza believed this, too. In the streets of Montevideo, they speak of it. At the Battle of Cerros Blancos, the tigers knew the hardness test for feldspar. I also would now know it: Can you scratch it with glass, but not a blade? What about topaz? Gypsum? If not, then feldspar, it is feldspar.

Then, the camping. For in the maze built by the Masked Dyer of Merv—for this was how I understood my Webelo Scout Book—it was also written: "Preparing and cooking your own meals outside is lots of fun. How good you feel, dishing up fine food that you have cooked over a campfire." If ever Paracelsus's spirit was with me, it was the day I read that passage! Keats, Shakespeare, J.F.K., they all shared that fine food.

On my campfire, I cooked hot dogs. Dogs, Mr. Wilkerson called them. Dogs. Then we made s'mores! We were dishing them up. How good I felt indeed!

The other children looked upon me strangely, though, hollow eyed. Their scarves were dirty. Their dreams were of Wheelies and scooters, of beating up pretentious "freaks" who used multisyllabic philosophical references in everyday conversation. I dreamt of effervescence. They giggled and poked my soon-scalding back with their ember-tipped, marshmallow-covered sticks. Stop it you assholes, I meekly whimpered. They only laughed more.

The next morning, with a mirror and an encyclopedia and the secrets of Dante, I began my new work. We were to build a small wood-planked bridge along a footpath in the woods. I, seeking the world between the visible and the serene, drew up plans for this bridge. My fellow scouts rejected it, of course, laughing yet more. Danny, little Danny, his Dale Jr. hat cocked, his heart blacker than a jaguar's, his ridicule was sharpest. We'd had a sleepover before—his mom made him, I know, but I thought we really connected.

From the half-light of dawn to the half-light of evening I worked on my bridge. When I returned from a side trip to watch the meadow's green spine, at the foot of my proud bridge stood Mr. Wilkerson. He had a riddle, I suspected, like a gatekeeper. He was passionate. About things larger than I'd known. About basketball. About chew. About OTB.

He asked, with the simplicity masking profundity I'd come to expect, "George"—for he called me George, even when I told him directly, I am Borges!—"the other kids finished their footbridges in about two hours. Your bridge is just a pile of split boards." Yes, I muttered, yes, he sees it all. "And the boards look like, did you, do they all have leaves stapled to them? George, what the f?"

Mr. Wilkerson, I knew, was leading to something larger than he or I. He muttered, not even directly to me. He spoke to the ground, as if to the Skoal he spit by his feet.

"Georgie boy, I can't, I just, you know I only do this because of Chip. I wish I could just go watch the damn game is all. And now you've got me dealing with all this crap? You've got to get a move on, Georgie. We can't leave until you've got this one done and done."

I consulted my Chinese calendar. I flipped open the map my local Cartographer's Guild made. I sat down and ate my PB&J. The other children frolicked. Mr. Wilkerson wept.

Ad Majorum Dei Gloriam, I whispered. He paused, pretending not to understand. Then he kicked the dirt clumps by the hollow in the tree I'd assembled in the order of Averroes's plans.

"What the hell are you saying, kid? Just, for crissakes, grab your wood and let me nail those together. Where is Chip? Chip, get over here and bring your hammer? Yes, sorry—no, it's George again. I know. He's gone once we get back. This is the last time. I promise."

I want to say it's Borges, the other one, these things happen to.

But into my juice box I weep silently: I am Borges.

A SERIES OF LETTERS TO HOMER FROM THIMINES, ODYSSEUS'S COLLEGE ROOMMATE

by William Hughes

Dear Great and Revered Speaker of Truths,

I'll preface this by saying I'm a big fan. Huge fan. Your stuff blows away everything else in the world of epic poetry. Gilga-who? Atra-huh-sis? Enuma E-whatever? Exactly.

And *The Iliad*? Fantastic! (Even though you forgot to mention that Odysseus got the idea for the Trojan Horse from me. Seriously! While we were living together, back in the dorms, I used to sort of have a thing for model glue, and one day I totally told him, "Oh, Odie, man [we used to call him Odie], we should build something with this stuff. We should build...a horse!" And then we laughed for like five hours. Bam, twenty years later, Trojan Horse. I bet you can't wait to update *The Iliad* to let people know about how I saved Greece!)

Anyway, I'm writing because I had a few questions about your new thing, *The Odyssey*, or whatever you're calling it. I caught a recitation last night by some blind guy, and I wanted you to know that this guy was really screwing the pooch. His version of it totally sucked! I mean, I think he added all of this extra, editorial stuff about how wise and noble Odie was, and about how brave he was, and he really seemed to be sending the wrong message to the kids in the audience.

And I know that you, oh great author, would never write a poem that celebrated a dude whose big claim to fame was getting lost and screwing around with a bunch of scantily clad "enchantresses" for twenty years. You and I both know that that's not what the common Greek on the street wants to hear! Nobody wants to listen to a story about how a guy who never managed above a 3.0 GPA is the "king of cunning," or hear lies about how the dude who had this wicked ugly case of back acne freshman year is now scoring with every hot chick in the Mediterranean. They want to hear about regular Joes. Guys like you and me!

So, I expect that as soon as you get this you'll fire that other guy doing the recitations before he can blow your reputation. Don't be too hard on him, though; he just doesn't know what makes good poetry the way you and I do, Mr. H!

Your Alpha-One Fan,
Thimines
Fisherman, Athens

P.S.: Also, I look forward to hearing the new version of *The Iliad*. I can't wait to tell my wife that I'm in a Homer!

Dear Great Storyteller,

You must think I'm a real dope for not realizing that it was YOU doing the recitation I heard last week. I know I do! And yeah, I guess it seems weird that a big fan like me wouldn't know you were blind, but I just try not to get caught up on appearances, you know?

But I really appreciate you writing me back and answering my questions about *The Odyssey*, even though I thought the tone of your letter was a little...cool. I guess whoever you dictate your letters to must have changed your words around before they sent it out! You should look into that, maybe fire that guy.

I guess I can see what you mean about how all the glory and the violence and the sex of Odie's little screwup make for good "storytelling." But what about the moral cost, yeah? What does it say to our kids that, of all the captains that came back from Troy, most of whom headed straight home and never once cheated on their wives, the one who gets the big damn poem is the one who leaves a trail of rumpled bedsheets and severed heads from here to Elysium?

I have an idea, though, that will help you save your poem, Mr. H. You just need to create a foil for Odysseus, a contrasting character, a man of virtue, a carpenter or a butcher or maybe a fisherman. Someone who would never cheat on his midterms like certain guys I could talk about and only gets drunk once or twice a week and never, ever cheats on his wife, even though she's plumped up a little bit these last couple of years and he has had PLENTY OF OPPORTUNITIES with that flirty little barmaid down at the local watering hole.

That way, your listeners have someone to identify with, and you don't have to worry about alienating them by making a guy like Odysseus— great guy, I love him like a brother, you know, but he can be kind of a dick—your hero.

Hope this helps, and I can't wait to hear the new version!

Your Biggest Fan,
Thimines
Fisherman, Athens

P.S.: Caught a reading of *The Iliad* last night, and didn't hear any mention of the Trojan Horse thing. I guess it takes a while to get the new version out!

Homer,

I was delighted to hear that you write your own letters, without using dictation. It's nice to see a person with disabilities rising to the task, you know?

It's less nice to find out that my favorite author can't handle a little constructive criticism. No, I DO NOT expect you to change the title of the work to *The Thiminessy*, as you so snidely suggested. I may just be a "stupid fisherman," but I know sarcasm when I read it, Mr. "I'm a legendary poet and you're just some schmuck." I just thought that a writer as GREAT as yourself would appreciate a little inside information, a little perspective, on one of his subjects.

Your "masterpiece" doesn't once mention, for instance, that Odysseus had a snore that would have put Aeolus to shame. Two years we lived together in that crappy little one-bedroom loft, and not once did I get a decent night's rest. But now, you never hear about that. Instead, it's cunning this, and brave and steadfast that, and nary a mention of the big old stink-eye he'd give you if you came home late and maybe you'd had a few drinks and you were being a little loud, and Olympus forbid you wake up King Odie the Judgmental and interrupt his evening's snore-fest.

But I guess you're not interested in objective storytelling, are you? No, it's all about the shock value for the "great" Homer. Zeus knows it would kill you to break up chapter after chapter of eyeball gougings and cannibalism to present the simple life of a kind, decent fisherman and his lovely wife. A simple human moment isn't good enough for the great sage, not when there's tales of philandering and murder to be told!

You make me sick, sir. Sick and full of pity.

Your former fan,
Thimines
Fisherman, Athens.

P.S.: Not that I would listen to your swill, but my friends tell me
there's still no mention of my contribution in *The Iliad.* Expect a
letter from my cousin Repidites, the lawyer, soon.

Hey Blind-O!

On my friends' recommendation, I caught your new version of *The Iliad*
last night. Was not amused by Thinimes, Odysseus's new sidekick, who,
as you well know, "smells of dead fish and a dead mind, lacking in all
virtues, whiny to a fault. Full of nattering questions, pale in the shadow
of the great Odysseus." Har de har! And you were really channeling
the great comedians when Thinimes, after falling down and crapping
himself every two minutes for the first three hours of the poem, gets a
spear through his crotch just as he's about to enter Troy. And then two
more spears through his arms, and then another one, with the word
"IDIOT" carved on it, in his head.

You must think you're pretty damn funny, buddy, but the last joke
is going to be on you. I know guys. Guys who do not care about the oral
tradition of epic poetry and its influences on world history. Guys who
are dead to the beauties of dactylic hexameter or innovative narrative
structures. In fact, they're pretty much indifferent to everything but
hurting wise-ass poets in exchange for a year's supply of fresh fish.

Watch your back, poet-boy. Oh wait, you can't.

Coming to get you,
Thimines
Fisherman, Athens

P.S.: *The Batrachomyomachia* sucked, and so do you.